Tippett, Alan Richard.
Church growth and the word of God : the
Biblical basis of the church growth
viewpoint /

Church Growth
and the Word of God

The Biblical Basis of the
Church Growth Viewpoint

by

A. R. TIPPETT

WILLIAM B. EERDMANS PUBLISHING COMPANY
GRAND RAPIDS, MICHIGAN

Copyright © 1970 by William B. Eerdmans Publishing Co.
All rights reserved
Library of Congress Catalog Card Number: 75-80877
ISBN 0-8028-1328-3
Printed in the United States of America

First printing, April 1970
Second printing, August 1974

Contents

Introduction: "So Were the Churches Established. . . ."   7

I   CHURCH GROWTH AS A BIBLICAL CONCEPT   9
    The Biblical Idea of Diffusion   10
    The New Testament Imagery of Growth   12
    Numbering: Right or Wrong?   15
    Obedience and Responsibility   18
    Conversion and Mission   19
    The Continuity and End of Growth   25

II   THE DYNAMICS OF CHURCH GROWTH   28
    The Biblical Awareness of Social Structure   28
    Growth by Multi-Individual Decision   31
    The Convert and His Context   33
    Acceptance and Rejection   37
    Functional Roles and Ingathering   40
    The Noncultural Factor   42

III   PROBLEMS OF NON-GROWTH   47
    Unpossessed Possessions   47
    Obstructing the Work of God   50
    The Principle of Strategic Location   52
    Service and Mission   54

IV   CHURCH GROWTH AND THE CURRENT SITUATION   58
    Belonging and the Process of Incorporating   58
    Perfecting Growth   61
    The Outreaching Church   64
    Organic Growth as Revitalization   67
    The Christian Mission Set in Time   71

V   CHURCH GROWTH AND THE CHRISTIAN HOPE   74
    The Promises of God   74
    The Church and the Consummation   77

Acknowledgments

From 1965 to 1967 some of the material in this book appeared in the *Church Growth Bulletin* of the School of World Mission and Institute of Church Growth, Fuller Theological Seminary. Dr. Donald A. McGavran, Dean of the School and Institute, as well as others have encouraged me to develop that material into the present form. The Reverend Roy E. Shearer has worked it over critically, checking all the references. I am grateful to these men for their encouragement and labors.

— A.R.T.

Introduction

The Lord's purpose, that knowledge of his love for mankind should be diffused throughout all nations, is well attested in the Old Testament, especially in the Psalms and in some of the Prophets. Some of the Lord's promises were realized historically with the coming of Christ. Others assumed shape with the emergence of the organic Church, a process that had already begun in New Testament times.

When the New Testament Church emerged, it was immediately quantitatively, qualitatively, and organically a *growing* body (Acts 2:46-7, 16:5). It assumed many forms, from house churches (I Cor. 16:19; Rom. 16:5; Col. 4:15; Philem. v. 2) and village communal units, as at Lydda and Saron (Acts 9:35), to mixed urban groups, as at Corinth (Acts 18:7-8), migrating groups and individuals, as at Rome (Rom. 16), and inter-racial segments at Roman colonial posts like Philippi (Acts 16).

Everywhere it quickly assumed an organized pattern. We read of elders (called, ordained, and held responsible, Acts 14:23, 20:17; Jas. 5:14), of overseers who feed the Church of God (Acts 20:28), and of the conceptualization of an ultimate general assembly (*panegurei*, Heb. 12:23). The Church had its messengers (II Cor. 8:23), chosen by responsible congregations to travel (v. 19). Various tasks were assigned to particular persons — "caring for the churches" (II Cor. 11:28; I Tim. 3:5), "confirming the Church" (Acts 15:41), "edifying the Church" (I Cor. 14:4,12). All this reflects growth on all levels — quantitative, qualitative, and organic. A terminology for the Church as the "Body of Christ" had been developed within a few years of the Lord's physical departure (Eph. 1:23; I Cor. 12:27; Rom. 12:4-5; Col. 1:18,24).

7

The driving power behind this activity of the Church was the Holy Spirit. It was the Holy Spirit who acted at Pentecost (Acts 2) and also in congregational decisions like those made at Antioch (Acts 13:2). It was the Holy Spirit who by commendation and warning henceforth spoke to all the churches through each of the churches (Rev. 2:7,11,17,29; 3:6,13,22).

This little book attempts to outline the biblical foundations of church growth. It seeks to show that the Church established by Jesus Christ and talked about in the Bible is and must continue to be a growing Church. The evidence is drawn from the hopes of Israel and the promises of God given of old to Israel, as stated in the Old Testament, and passes from them to the messages given to the Church, as heir of the promises, in the New Testament. These messages, together with appropriate warnings and specific directions for mission, are found in the teachings of Jesus and his apostles under the guidance of the Holy Spirit. The instructions to the Church were set down in such passages as the Great Commission (Matt. 28:18-20), the statement of the apostolic principle, based on Christ's own apostleship to the world (John 17:18), the direct claim of Christ that he is alone the way to the Father (John 14:6), and the restatement of the apostolic responsibility to witness and incorporate converts into the fellowship (I John 1:1-3).

I

Church Growth as a Biblical Concept

The evidence from Scripture for this study is *declarative, implicative, precedential,* or *cumulative.*

By *declarative evidence* I mean a direct, specific, or categorical statement or an imperative. "Go ye therefore into all the world. . . ." "As my Father hath sent me into the world even so send I you into the world." "Grace and truth came by Jesus Christ."

By *implicative evidence* I mean statements clearly implied in the passages cited. A figure of speech implies something that may or may not be stated directly. "Ye are the light of the world" implies that the world is dark and that the Christian has a specific role in that darkness, though it does not actually say so. The integrity of the meaning of the passage depends on the implication of the imagery.

By *precedential evidence* I mean that God has shown his approval of, and set his Spirit on, say, the method of the Antioch missionary program, because it is an historic case recorded in Scripture. Even if it does not say that this shall thereafter be God's method, the fact that he once blessed it indicates that it is in accord with his will at least for some situations. This is evidence by precedence.

By *cumulative evidence* I mean the quantitative assembly of scriptural statements that point in a single direction and reinforce each other. Thus, for example, many passages of Scripture refer to the sacrifice of Christ, his atonement for sin, and his role as burden-bearer, though perhaps they do not actually use the word "love." Nevertheless such a corpus of material demonstrates his great love for man. Cumulative evidence demonstrates truth by its reinforcing abundance.

9

THE BIBLICAL IDEA OF DIFFUSION

In his *History of Protestant Missions,* the great theorist of missions, G. Warneck, seeks for the historic rediscovery of the idea of Christian mission that the Church had lost by the time of the Reformation. Even during the Reformation, the Reformers, in their struggle to establish themselves against Rome, could not see beyond their *"Reformation* mission" within their particular historical context. It was left for the Pietists to stress the *Christian* mission. Yet all along that idea was quite clear in the Bible.

In Scripture the Christian mission to the heathen is not merely going forth, with the emphasis on *obedience;* it is also, in scriptural promise and action, the diffusion of the knowledge of salvation to the ends of the earth.

The Psalmists sing the praise and salvation of God to "the ends of the earth" (a phrase that appears about ten times in the Psalms) and to the "uttermost parts" (2:8, 65:8). "All the nations" shall call him blessed (72:17). This idea of the worship of the *nations* appears about fifteen times in the Psalms, and it is to the *nations* that this salvation is to be dispensed (67:2). The Psalms leave us in no doubt about God's purpose. Reverence for the Lord is to be worldwide, with kings and rulers bowing at his feet (2:10-11). He is King of all the earth (47:8) and due for worship by "the families of the nations" when they turn to the Lord (22:27-8). He is Savior, Judge, and Guide and due for praise (67:3-7). Israel is responsible for declaring the glory of God to the nations that he alone may rule and that idols be done away with (96:1-13).

This expectation of diffusion was shared by the prophets, who saw "the house of prayer" as "for all people" (Isa. 56:7), and the significance of the gathering of the nations (Jer. 3:17). The Gentiles would know the greatness of his name (Mal. 1:11), for he is "the desire of all nations" (Hag. 2:7), the source of peace for the heathen (Zech. 9:10), and the light unto the Gentiles (Isa. 42:6, 60:3, etc.). The idea of salvation diffused as light in darkness appears about a dozen times in Isaiah alone. So the good news is seen in the imagery of health, light, peace, desire, salvation, as knowledge of the Lord (Hab. 2:14), and as incorporation into the house of prayer (Isa. 56:7) — all as a promised diffusion.

In Isaiah 56:6-8 Jehovah, "who gathers the outcasts of Israel," speaks of "foreigners who join themselves to the Lord," who accept the pattern of worship and are incorporated into it, making it a "house of prayer for all peoples," and he concludes by promising to "gather yet others." In several places in the Psalms the same thing is implied where God is being praised by individuals and nations "in the sanctuary" (Psa. 96:6; 134:2; 150:1). Thus the Old Testament speaks not only of a diffusion of the good news about God but of a believing, praising, praying community. The *congregation* as a group with whom one prays and praises and gives testimony is well known in the Psalms (22:22,25; 35:18; 40:9-10; 107:32; 111:1, etc.).

What the Old Testament speaks, the New Testament confirms. Christ is the Light of the *world* (John 8:12). Many verses in both the Gospel and the Epistle of John support this in confirmation of the Isaiah promises. The love of God is for the *world* (3:16). The prophetic passages cited are identified with Christ (e.g. Matt. 4:16), and converts beyond the immediate audience are to be incorporated into the flock (John 10:16). The glorious life, death, and resurrection of the Lord culminate with the Great Commission to go to all *nations* (Matt. 28:19). Our Lord and his recorders confirmed the concept of diffusion spoken of earlier — "the earth shall be full of the knowledge of the Lord as the waters cover the sea" (Isa. 11:9, a messianic passage).

Acting on these Old Testament promises and their confirmation by the Lord himself, the young Church planted churches by missionary journeys, preaching and teaching. They testified of Christ, and incorporated converts into the fellowship (I John 1:1-3); and the New Testament, as it comes to us, has as its grand finale the picture of the ultimate consummation, when old things are passed away and all things are new (Rev. 21:4-5), and Christ is established as the light (21:24) and healing (22:2) of the nations in the frame of reference of a worshipping community.

The whole Bible vibrates with expectancy — from the psalmist and prophet to the evangelist and apostle and the Lord himself. Of those engaged in the program of Christian mission today, obedience is surely required — but it is *expectant* obedience. If the Bible still speaks to us, it surely speaks of the diffusion of the salvation experience, and the incorporation of the saved into a fellowship.

We need to keep this in mind in a day when "the mission of the Church" is sometimes reduced to mere dialog, to service projects or to the fight for social justice. We are not denying the rightness of any of these worthy programs. We fully recognize them as necessary to the true and essential outworkings of the gospel. But they are no *substitute* for the diffusion of the salvation experience and for the incorporation into a fellowship of those who have experienced salvation. It is indeed only by the strengthening and maturing of young converts in such a fellowship that they are able to go forth and apply their new experience in the world, in terms either of encounter or of service. Thus Jesus established his practice of taking his disciples apart from the world for instruction and prayer that they might return in strength for service in the world.

We should note well that the fellowship of the physical group, the drawing aside from the persecution and burden of the Christian way in the world for instruction and prayer, was a *specific* part of Jesus' method. Matthew 20:17 and Mark 6:31, for instance, say quite clearly that the "Christian presence" alone is not enough without the reinforcement of the fellowship. We are not denying the Christian's burden in the world; but we are saying that he cannot adequately perform this servant role and the apostolic role without a group experience of sharing, praying, and being instructed.

THE NEW TESTAMENT IMAGERY OF GROWTH

The attitude that we must expect slow growth distresses me. It is quite foreign to the New Testament, which, on the contrary, has a rich range of picturesque imagery that shows growth is to be expected — both physical, numerical growth from outside and spiritual, qualitative growth from within. The New Testament nouns and verbs leave no room for static causes.

The teaching of Jesus was charged with expectation of growth. It comes in so many different metaphors that they may well be classified into types. Here are some of them.

(1)   In the first place our Lord used a great deal of *quantitative imagery* — the man with the net catching fish (Matt. 13:47-8), the call of fishermen to become fishers of men (Mark 1:17), and the increasing bulk of the loaf under the influence of leavening (Matt. 13:33).

(2)   He also used the *imagery of ingathering,* such as his reference to fields "white unto harvest" (John 4:35) and allied expressions, the term "Lord of the harvest" (Matt. 9:38, Luke 10:2), and the direct commission that they were to pray for harvesters (Matt. 9:37-8).

(3)   The entity of the fellowship of the disciples that later expanded into the Church was to be nourished by a Christian experience. This was depicted in *imagery of interaction* in the allegory of the vine and the branches, the function of the branches being specifically to produce fruit (John 15:5, 8).

(4)   Our Lord also conceptualized the fellowship as a gathering of folk from outside. To this end he used the *imagery of incorporation,* as, for example, when he commissioned the ingathering of folk from the highways and hedges to the banquet (Luke 14:21-4). If such parables have any meaning at all, they point out that the fellowship should grow.

(5)   A great lover of nature and an observer of its processes, the Lord did not hesitate to draw his illustrations as *organic imagery* of emerging life and growth about him. He dwelt on the concept of the growing seed; he saw the tiny mustard seed becoming a mighty tree (Matt. 13:31-2, etc.).

(6)   In the same way he used the figure of light. Here he conceptualized his gospel of truth in the *imagery of penetration* — the light penetrates the darkness. Jesus himself was the Light (John 8:12, 9:5). He also called his followers to be the light, bringing men to glorify God (Matt. 5:16).

The apostles followed the methods of communication and reasoning patterns of the Lord, using some of his imagery and innovating more for themselves.

The leaders of the early Church developed further this concept of light penetrating the darkness — Paul (II Cor. 4:6),

Peter (II Pet. 1:19), and John (I John 1:7, etc.). Furthermore, the prologue of John's Gospel conceives the motive of Christ's coming to earth in terms of light penetration. Paul also saw his own missionary commission in terms of the penetrating light (Acts 26:18). The Church grows as the light spreads.

John also developed the idea of the group, conceptualizing the Christian fellowship as growing by the incorporation of those who were won as a result of the apostles' public witness (I John 1:3).

The imagery of Paul is worthy of special examination. He saw the technical construction work going on in the growing cities of the empire and used it to speak of the growth of the Church. Thus, in his architectural imagery we are reminded of the building of the house (I Cor. 3:9-11) and the building "fitly framed together, growing into a holy temple" (Eph. 2:22).

Paul also made use of *imagery of social structure,* like the family of God, growing by "the spirit of adoption" (Rom 8:15; Eph. 1:5).

None of these metaphors stands alone. In some way or other they all suggest development, growth, expansion, penetrating into the world, incorporating new people, multiplication, building, gains both qualitative and quantitative. As a cumulative collection of figures they indicate the broad perspective of the Master and his men. With them there is no room for the static.

The parable of the sower (Luke 8:5-8, 11-15) does not justify the inevitability of some non-growth, or permit any resignation to that inevitability. The purpose of the parable is to classify situations under which seed grows and does not grow, so that the intelligent farmer may be more sensible in his planting. He who made the seed surely did so that it might grow and multiply. In line with many of the parables of Jesus as preserved by Luke (e.g. those concerning the responsibility that goes with wealth), this is a warning to the servants of God. To the crowd gathered to hear him, Jesus said, "He that hath ears to hear let him hear" (v. 8). This is a warning against unresponsiveness. To the apostles, who later have the full explanation of why some reject the gospel and others accept, it seems to me that Jesus is saying that it is not enough to receive the word with joy; it must take root, or it will fail in the time of temptation (v. 13). If the seed is choked with cares, riches, and pleasures, it will not bear fruit to perfection (v. 14), implying that this is God's purpose for the planted seed. But if the seed falls on good ground, it will bring forth good fruit with patience (v. 15). Why "with patience"? This implies the ultimate purpose for growth. Surely this is implicative evidence for the importance of seed-planting in responsive soil.

Numbering: Right or Wrong?

A certain scholar disturbs me by declaring that church growth statistical comparisons are unscriptural, on the basis of David's punishment for numbering Israel (I Chron. 21). His view is that the work is God's; we merely have to be obedient. Let us discuss that narrative a little.

After a series of military victories, David was provoked by Satan to number Israel (v. 1). Such temptation was possible because David was now proudly aware of his kingdom and his military strength and organization. The numbering was a sin because it was self-glorification. This is implied by the fact that the count was taken of the fighting men (v. 5). Both Joab and David knew it was wrong (v. 3). It was also wrong because it failed to recognize that Israel's strength was in the arm of the Lord (vv. 9-13). David's motive for the numbering was quite wrong, and the Lord humbled him on this account. The penitent David sacrificed to the Lord (vv. 26-27) and turned from self-glorification to begin plans for building the House of the Lord (I Chron. 22:1ff.).

But how then can we account for another occasion on which God specifically directed a numbering at Sinai (Num. 1:17-19)? Here Israel was to be organized into families and lineages, and in this way the people were to be recorded in order that none be lost in the wilderness (2:32-34). In the same way God directed a second numbering in Moab (Num. 26:1-4), organized in the same sociological categories as the first, to demonstrate that all of the former numbering (except Caleb and Joshua) had perished in the wilderness and lost their inheritance through their lack of faith (26:63-65).

Satan provoked David to use numbering to reinforce a false
sense of security in human strength. David's motive was wrong,
and he was justly humiliated as a result. However, God *directed*
Moses to demonstrate certain facts by numbering. Here the
motive was right.

In certain parables (Luke 15) our Lord used the statistical
principle for preserving the unity of the whole. The shepherd
had one hundred sheep in his flock. It was an exact count.
He therefore knew that one solitary sheep was missing, as did
the woman who had lost the coin from her string of ten. The
awareness of the loss led to the searching, finding, and con-
sequent rejoicing; but all this was possible only because of
accurate counting. The motive of numbering here is pastoral
care.

Missionary Miller of Korea discussed the problem of shrink-
age in church membership due to removal or wandering. Its
discovery and correction depends on correct counting and
recording. Church statistics ask questions and demand answers.
They demonstrate facts that require urgent notice. The Good
Shepherd knows his sheep, even by name (John 10:3).

I noted on one of my field trips that, in the statistics of a
certain mission, a figure of 2500 reappeared year after year.
It was obviously a rough estimate in the first place, and the
missionary responsible had simply carried it forward each year.
The shepherd did not know how many sheep he had. He did
not know how many were in the fold and how many lost in
the wilderness.

The motive for the careful numbering required in mission
statistics is not pride in our accomplishments but the recognition of the seriousness of the commission given to us lesser
shepherds to "care for the flock of God" until "the Chief Shepherd comes" (I Pet. 5:2-4). Good numbering is part of good
shepherding.

At the beginning (Luke 5:1-14) and the end (John 21:1-13)
of our Lord's earthly ministry, we find accounts of miraculous
draughts of fish. The occasions and purposes of the recording evangelists are not the same. In detail there are some
similarities; but there are also some striking differences. On
the first occasion, Simon was brought to see himself as a sin-

ner, to make his confession, and to receive the call to become a fisher of men (Luke 5:8-10). On the second occasion, after the initial excitement because "it was the Lord," Simon proved himself the practical disciple who actually drew the net to land and made an exact count of the catch (John 21:11). Furthermore, the evangelist thought it worth recording these statistical details and adding the comment "yet was not the net broken." The fellowship of Master and men, broken through the Lord's crucifixion and burial, was restored so that the disciples, through this miracle, knew "that it was the Lord" (v. 12). That such an otherworldly event should be recorded with such worldly details — "Catch: 153 fish" — arrests the thoughtful reader. The commonplace information is surely provided, not for its own sake, but as evidence of the power of God at work in the miracle.

In church growth research the statistics are never presented as an end in themselves. This would disqualify them by definition. If the motivation for numbering is self-glorification or denominational glorification, it stands biblically condemned, as the precedent of David illustrates. In church growth research, however, statistics are examined as evidence of the state of the Lord's work — where it is prospering or where something is obstructing its growth — that it may be applied to a self-examination of the techniques of our stewardship or shepherding in all humility. We seek to discover where these techniques may be improved, that God's name alone may be praised. To condemn the church growth method on the basis of a generalization "that quality counts more than quantity" is unsound, unfair, and unkind. It is sound scriptural method to assume that leadership should be tested now, because ultimately it will stand before the judgment of God. Thus, numerical data are of value to us, and we are responsible for keeping mission statistics with care.

Our statistical records may be used for comparison, as at Sinai and Moab; or for indicating where sheep have strayed from the flock that they may be sought and found again; or as part of the practical follow-up of ingathering, as Simon the fisherman hauled in the catch and recorded it carefully after the initial excitement of meeting the Lord.

OBEDIENCE AND RESPONSIBILITY

The theme of God's sovereignty and man's obedience keeps recurring in the Christian mission. No true missionary would deny it. Yet often we isolate these concepts from one another and thereby make them half-truths. Obedience never stands alone. The undeniably right idea of God's sovereignty and our obedience can be abused when man is seen as a *mere instrument* in God's hand and not in any way a *responsible agent*. It is therefore important and biblical to stress this second concept in the Christian mission.

Paul sees man as a *co-worker* with God (I Cor. 3:9: literally, fellow-worker, *sunergoi;* and II Cor. 6:1, where the same word is used in the verbal form), a concept implied throughout the New Testament imagery. With the role of the co-worker goes the requirement of responsibility.

In several of the Lord's parables, such as the parables of the pounds (Luke 19:11-28) and the talents (Matt. 25:14-30), the recipient of the gift is a responsible agent — i.e., responsible for the correct use of the gift. Ultimately the Lord's appraisal is based on the good and faithful use of the gift. Note especially Matthew 25:26-7, where the servant is judged for irresponsibility.

When Jesus was calling, instructing, and commissioning his servants, he used imagery that implied both special knowledge and responsibility. The picture was always one of responsible co-workers — the vinedresser (Luke 13:6-9), fishers of men (Matt. 4:19), harvesters (John 4:35), and servants for the feast (Matt. 22:8-10). All of these workmen knew the right and wrong ways of using the techniques of their respective occupations — they were responsible agents. Their duty to obey the will of the master implied that they did so within their own specialized methods.

Paul also was alert to the responsibility of the human agent in the Christian life and mission. Conceptualizing the role of man as that of a builder, he said, "Let every man take heed how he buildeth." The foundation is provided for us, but we build and are responsible (I Cor. 3:10-13).

Elsewhere Paul saw the Christian life and mission as a conflict with the forces of evil. We are responsible soldiers (Eph.

6:11-18). In one passage he used three figures — the soldier, the athlete, and the farmer — to urge Timothy to commit the task of the Christian mission to reliable, or faithful men (II Tim. 2:2-6).

The apostle Peter, remembering his own commission, "Feed my lambs! Feed my sheep!" (John 21:15-7), also preserved this concept of pastoral responsibility. To the leaders of the Church he said, "Feed the flock of God which is among you, taking the oversight thereof..." (I Pet. 5:2); and he pointed out that our oversight is subject to inspection and appraisal when the Chief Shepherd shall come (v. 4). Surely this is a pastoral application of his Master's parables of the pounds and talents.

The church growth viewpoint stresses the obedience of man, but it is obedience within a context of responsibility. The human role in this mission to mankind is not mechanical but personal. It implies the existence of special God-given gifts, knowledge of techniques, and responsibility for proficiency. If God sees his *sunergoi* as cultivators, builders, soldiers, fishermen, harvesters, and shepherds, then we may assume that he has provided the resources and expects us to use them wisely and well as we build his Church under the direction of his Spirit.

Certainly he is sovereign, and we should be obedient — that refers to the will. Equally true, we are his co-workers, and therefore we are responsible — that refers to the administration of the techniques and specialized knowledge of our calling. It is to understand this better and to use it more effectively that church growth research has been established.

CONVERSION AND MISSION

Church growth occurs with the process of conversion. We are concerned with statistical growth that is based on conversion intake. The New Testament assumes that a man becomes a Christian by the act of conversion. This is a clear about-face.

There are two scriptural ways of regarding conversion. Basically it is an act of God. God, through his Spirit, strives with man, convicts him of sin, and assures him of salvation (Rom. 8:14-16; I Cor. 2:9-14; Eph. 2:4-5). When we think of conversion as men being saved (Eph. 2:8), of "adding to the Church daily such as should be saved" (Acts 2:47), as men obtaining eternal life (John 3:15-17, 10:25) or becoming new creatures (II Cor. 5:17), we are thinking of what God alone can do for man. This is looking at the divine side of the conversion experience.

But there is a human side which concerns us greatly in the Christian mission. Man has to be brought to surrender his will to God's. He has to respond, or "to second the motion of the Holy Spirit," as Wesley put it. From the human side, man decides for Christ, or a tribe of people accepts Christ. This is an act of human volition and of major significance in the theology of mission.

The human side of conversion is described in the New Testament by a set of strong action verbs which throw responsibility for decision on the convert. He is presented with an option for acceptance or rejection. The way of grace is open to all, and it is not the will of God that man should perish. But man himself must respond. Repeated refusal is the sin against the Holy Spirit (Matt. 12:31), and the eternal consequences of such refusal make the Christian mission urgent (II Cor. 6:1-2). This human aspect of conversion is expressed in four ways — *turning to the Lord, repenting, confessing,* and *believing.*

(1) Etymologically, *turning to the Lord* is the true meaning of "conversion." It is used in reference to individuals or groups, and often in association with "believing" or "repenting." All who dwelt at Lydda and Saron "turned to the Lord" at one time (Acts 9:36). "Repent and be converted," Peter urged his hearers in his first great sermon on Pentecost (Acts 3:19, where the Greek word for "be converted" is not passive, but the active "turn"). Confronted by the effective preaching of the Cypriots at Antioch, the Grecians "believed and turned unto the Lord" (Acts 11:21). Lydda and Saron were village communities; the Grecians were an ethnic segment. There are also passages in Acts where the biblical historian speaks of "the turning of the tribes" (15:3) and "those of the tribes turning to God" (15:19).

The corollary of this, as Paul pointed out (I Thess. 1:9), is that turning to God also means turning away from idols. This is real conversion. Paul regarded his role as the preaching of this message, to show the tribes that "they should repent and turn to God" (Acts 26:20).

In his last words to the Jews at Rome, Paul quoted from the Old Testament to show how hardness of heart can lead to rejection of the offer of salvation, and here again for "conversion" he used the word "turn" (Acts 28:27; cf. John 12:37-40).

(2) The Gospel account of the life and work of Christ is heralded by a prophetic call to *repent* (Matt. 3:2, 4:17; Mark 1:15). This was also the burden of the first preaching of the disciples (Mark 6:12). In the synoptics this word has some theological depth. Repentance is the human side of conversion (an attitude toward sin), as the remission of sin is the divine side. The two aspects are stated together (Mark 1:4; Luke 3:3, 24:47). The conversion (repenting) of the sinner is a matter for rejoicing in heaven (Luke 15:7, 10); but, on the other hand, Jesus left us in no doubt about the tragic fate of the man who refused to repent (Matt. 11:20-24; Luke 11:29,32; 13:3,5).

In the Acts of the Apostles, Peter used the same relationship between repentance and remission of sins (Acts 2:38), the blotting out of sin (3:19), or its forgiveness (8:22). Both Peter and Paul linked repenting with turning to God (3:19, 26:20).

(3) The idea of *confessing* Christ originated in the preaching of Jesus himself (Matt. 10:32; Luke 12:8); however, his preaching also included the sad possibility of a man choosing the alternative option of denying him and thereby paying the price (Matt. 10:33; Luke 12:9). John pointed out that confessing Christ might lead to unpleasant reactions on earth (John 9:22), but that a faithful confession on our part would be honored by him who is faithful and just and forgives sin (I John 1:9), and brings us into divine fellowship (I John 4:15). The same Greek word is used for "confessing" Christ as for "confessing" one's sin.

Paul also presented the idea of confessing Christ, and linked it with believing — confessing with the mouth and believing with the heart (Rom. 10:9-10). The idea of Christ himself as a missionary to man seeking conversion is found in the great self-emptying passage (Phil. 2:5-11), the aim being "that every tongue should confess."

In the great conversion movement among the exorcists of
Ephesus, when many believed, confessed, exposed their magical
arts (Acts 19:18), and destroyed paraphernalia to the value of
fifty thousand pieces of silver (v. 19), there was the conversion
of a large segment of a craft community. Here again we find
this combination of confessing and believing (v. 18).

(4) Jesus called people to *believe* (Mark 5:36; John 9:35-38,
etc.). In John's Gospel, witnessing to bring men to belief is a
basic principle (1:7, 5:24, 17:20-21). Indeed, his Gospel was
written for this express purpose (20:31). The key to grace, the
power to become sons of God, and the way to eternal life is by
believing (1:12; 3:15-16,36; 6:47); and this is the will of God
(6:40). Both the evangelist and Jesus, whom he cites, are concerned with the lostness of man, the possibility of deliberate
unbelief, and its tragic consequences (3:15-20; 10:25-26; 16:8-9).
Those who believe and respond to the Shepherd's call are of the
flock; those who do not respond are not his sheep (10:26-27).
He who believes "is passed from death unto life" (5:24). This
is conversion.

Even before the revelation was complete, many people began to believe in Jesus (John 7:31; 8:30; 10:42): Jews (8:21;
12:11), Samaritans (4:39), and even some of the rulers (12:42).
The latter, however, did not confess openly — an interesting
qualification. By the end of his ministry, Jesus was drawing
together a company of believing persons (17:8), and when this
belief had extended to the resurrection (20:8-9, 20:27-29) they
were almost ready for the task of the Christian mission. Then
came Pentecost.

In Acts, the distribution of believers was extended. From
Acts 2:5-11, we may assume that these early converts included
Jews, proselytes, "strangers of Rome," Cretans, and Arabians.
In Iconium the converts were Jews and Greeks (14:1), and
also in Corinth (18:4); yet Paul adds (v. 8) that many Corinthians believed. The believing centurions (10:24, 44-8) were
undoubtedly Romans. The Greeks of Antioch were introduced
to the faith by men of Cyprus and Cyrene (11:20-21, a passage
which couples the terms "believing" and "turning to the
Lord"). Thus the process of growth in the early Church was by

adding believers to the Lord (5:14, 11:24) from all social and ethnic groups.

Some conversion stories were about individuals; but conversion movements among different groups of people are common in Acts, and some occurred in large mixed crowds. There were three thousand at Pentecost (2:41), and five thousand "heard and believed" after the preaching of Peter and John (4:4). The group movement under Philip's preaching in Samaria was recorded in terms of believing (8:12), as was the individual conversion of the Ethiopian (8:37) and the conversion of the household group at Philippi (16:31-32). In this case, note that the word of the Lord was presented to the whole group (v. 32), not to the jailer alone; all were baptized (v. 33), and all believed (v. 34). The coupling of the human act in conversion (believing) with the divine act (remission of sin) is found in Acts in the preaching of Peter to Cornelius and his kinsmen (10:43). The Roman had gathered his kinsmen and friends together to hear what Peter had to say. The Book of Acts confronts us with responsive and obstructive groups. In Pisidian Antioch, after Paul had given his message and a strong warning on the danger of unbelief, the people asked to hear the message again (13:42). Some (both Jews and proselytes) were already disposed to believe (v. 43), but on the following Sunday the real response came from the Gentiles (v. 48).

To pass from the conversion experiences of Acts to the developed theology of Romans, Paul conceptualizes conversion to salvation as believing (1:16, 3:22, 4:24, 6:8, 9:33, 10:4, 11), coupling believing and confessing (10:10). Stating first the need for conversion by believing (10:11), Paul goes on in a strong missionary passage to show the need for preaching to secure believing (vv. 14,17. Cf. I Cor. 1:21) and then warns against the tragedy of disobedience (10:19-21). As in Acts, this letter shows the motivation that the nations may be brought to faith (16:26).

Paul, though he uses the verbal action "believing" or "those who believe" quite frequently, nevertheless shows a strong preference for the noun "faith" from the same word cluster. It appears 140 times in his letters. This, however, is more the resultant state of the converted people. Conversion is an act of turning to the Lord and believing. When we enter this area of the spiritual state of the man of faith, the converted believer, or the community of them, we become involved in the nonquantitative aspect of church growth; this growth is manifested internally and externally in worship and instruction within the fellowship, and proclamation and social action outside in the world. We have passed from the conversion experience per se to the Christian life in action, to "fruits worthy of repentance" (Matt. 3:8).

What does the New Testament study of conversion say to Christian missions? I believe it speaks to the lostness of man, and it declares the responsibility of Christian man to proclaim Christ, that lost men everywhere may be converted. The Church grows by the conversion of men to Christ. The message has to be proclaimed for a verdict; men must turn to the Lord, with repenting, believing, and confessing. These are positive acts. Mere numerical growth without this is vain. Before statistics are used in church growth research, the preliminary question must always be asked: what do these figures actually represent?

The biblical study of conversion also shows that it is not enough for a Christian mission to be merely a "Christian presence" out there. This type of missioning moves toward coexistent indifference. It does not allow for the lostness of man and the responsibility of the Christian individual and Christian group to be concerned with the spiritual plight that lies behind the physical plight of the world. The Great Commission presupposes that God is willing to use men to bring men to Christ. Of course, only God can convert men, but he has been pleased to use the human agent for presenting to men the blessing of turning unto the Lord, and the dire consequences of rejecting it.

In the first baptisms mentioned in the New Testament, when John was operating at the Jordan, confessing and baptizing went together (Matt. 3:6; Mark 1:5). Jesus' words about the importance of believing and the danger of not believing (Mark 16:16) suggest that this believing should be demonstrated in public by an act of baptism. In the record of the New Testament Church in Acts we find believing associated with baptism. They are mentioned together in at least six episodes (8:13, 37-8; 11:16-17; 16:33-34; 18:8; 19:4-5).

While there is no scriptural foundation for any doctrine of baptismal regeneration, and conversion is by grace through faith alone, yet it certainly does seem that people coming out of paganism, or out of the world, should be received in an act of baptism. This is not only an entry into the fellowship group, but it is also a demonstration of one's confessing and believing. When people are converted and baptized in sufficient numbers, churches are planted and grow. There is no other way whereby the Church may grow but by conversion.

THE CONTINUITY AND END OF GROWTH

I have heard men allege that their church growth has stopped for a period of consolidation or quality growth. But quantitative and qualitative growth should proceed together. I hold with Sidney J. W. Clark, the prewar missionary strategist, that when a tree stops growing, it dies.

The biblical concept of growth, as far as it relates to the work of God, whether we think of it physically or qualitatively, is a continuous process until the final end.

Quantitatively, the Church is expected to grow in bulk and strength. The New Testament shows us the "adding to the Church daily" (Acts 2:46-7), the churches being established (16:5), and the need for intake into the fellowship (I John 1:3). In terms of preaching the word of the kingdom (Matt. 13:19), the conversions are measured even to a hundred-fold in some cases (v. 23). In terms again of the kingdom of heaven, we have the planting of the tiny mustard seed, its growth into a mighty tree, and the production of further seed (vv. 31-2). Or again, there is the figure of the ever-expanding loaf due to the presence of leaven (v. 33). This is what Dr. McGavran defines as "discipling" in his *Bridges of God,* following the Great Commission — *mathēteusate* — "Disciple ye." Always two things are noted: the growth itself and the growth to a specific end.

The incident of the barren fig tree (Matt. 21:19) reminds us of the tragedy of growth in bulk alone. The tree fails in its basic purpose — to produce fruit. There was good reason for judgment on the barren tree. If it fails to produce fruit at the appropriate season, it also fails to reproduce. This is not only a failure of service; it is also a failure to maintain the continuity of production: no fruit means no new plants, no more growing trees, the stoppage of the process. So the growing Church must have its program of outreach: service certainly, but also witness to maintain the continuity of the growth process itself. The cycle of recurring seasons — summer, winter, seedtime, and harvest — is built into life on earth by the laws of God (Gen. 8:22).

The symbol of growth is used also on the qualitative level — what McGavran calls "perfecting." We are expected to grow in grace and knowledge of Christ (II Pet. 3:18), to grow in the word (I Pet. 2:2), to grow up to maturity in Christ (Eph. 4:15), to grow in faith and love (II Thess. 1:3). These admonitions are based on the figure of the growth of the body from immaturity to maturity; but here again it is the need for continuity in perfection growth that is stressed.

Even when the idea of growth or building up is expressed in a mere image, such as the symbol of the construction of a building, it is always a building to a particular end. The man who builds a tower without proper planning, so that he does not reach the final goal, becomes a laughingstock (Luke 14:28-9). Jesus himself used the figure when he said he would build his Church on Peter's confession of faith (Matt. 16:18).

The same idea is developed by Paul — we are to be rooted and builded in Christ (Col. 2:7), fitly framed together, a holy temple, a habitation of God, through the Spirit (Eph. 2:21-2).

Peter also expressed the same concept in terms of a spiritual house built of living stones (I Pet. 2:4-5) in a passage about growth and the calling of Christians as the people of God. Quantitative and qualitative growth must both go on continuously to the establishment of more and more mature congregations (Acts 16:5).

Furthermore, this continuity of life, of seasons, of harvests, of building, of multiplication, must go on until Christ comes. As the house of Christ, we are to hold confidence and hope to the end (Heb. 3:6), to be steadfast to the end (v. 14), diligent and with full assurance to the end (6:11), confirmed to the end (I Cor. 1:8), fruitful in holiness to the end which is everlasting life (Rom. 6:22), enduring to the end (Mark 13:13).

There is no "letup" in this continuous program either at the discipling or perfecting levels. The Church's missionary program began with the first coming of our Lord and extends until his return. In the light of that certainty, Paul's benediction for the Thessalonians was for sanctification "unto the coming of our Lord Jesus Christ" (I Thess. 5:23).

When we remember that ultimate end, we see clearly the reason for the need of continuity of growth, both quantitative and qualitative.

II

The Dynamics of Church Growth

THE BIBLICAL AWARENESS OF SOCIAL STRUCTURE

If the gospel is to be universal and eternal, it must have the ability to operate in all kinds of social structures. It must speak to the national situations of all kinds of communities at each period of history and be meaningful within the limitations of all social units.

The delivery of God's word extended over thousands of years of history, during which time the dominant social structure changed from patriarchal society to oriental monarchy to empire. We are not told that one was right and another wrong, but that the word of God was relevant to all these situations, and that the "people of God" were to proclaim it.

"The word of the Lord came to Abram," we are told near the beginning of the Bible in the days of the nomadic, tent-dwelling community. In a later period, the psalms of David show the king's receptivity to "the word of the Lord" in times of both success and failure, of joy and depression. In their day the prophets proclaimed, "Thus saith the Lord!" Centuries later, in a very different social complex, "the residents of Asia heard the word of the Lord, both Jews and Greeks" (Acts 19:10). Thus, throughout these years of history and in all types of social structures, the word of the Lord "came through" to men. Cultural and historical differences did not prevent communication. God's word is not bound by time, place, or literary form. It has come to men in the poetry, prose, and verbal proclamation with which they have been familiar in their respective periods. He who spoke within the varied social

28

configurations of two thousand years of biblical history can
speak to the nations today.

The regular reader of the Old Testament is frequently aware
that God's word came through to people who lived and be-
haved within the limits of social patterns quite different from
his own. An anthropologist reading the last chapter of the
Book of Numbers, for instance, would recognize that here is an
account of the institution of a pattern of marriage choice —
prescribed parallel cousin marriage — and that the motivation
behind the custom was the preservation of the inheritance
within the tribe. For those people at that time in history, this
pattern apparently had the Lord's approval. Let the westerner
stop and consider that for a moment. The interpretation of the
ethics of Boaz' spreading his skirt over Ruth by night in the
field (Ruth 3:6ff.) depends on an understanding of the social
customs and laws of redemption within which this drama was
enacted. God's will and word came through to them within
that configuration.

God called the patriarchal lineage of Israel to recognize that
he alone saved them from Egypt and was to be their God
(Exod. 20:2-5). The structure and cohesion of a patriarchal
household was a built-in feature of the Ten Commandments:
son, daughter, man-servant, maid-servant, and the stranger
within the gates (vv. 10-17) were all the responsibility of the
patriarch of that structural social unit.

Israel as a nation was called (Isa. 43:1) after having been
redeemed, and then she was commissioned to witness before
the nations (vv. 9-10). Salvation was to be proclaimed (vv. 11-
12). As for Assyria, apparently that nation could be saved
without the necessity of changing her social structure. Repenting and turning to God would bring the promised salvation,
even within the pattern of absolute monarchy (Jonah 3). A
phrase in Zephaniah speaks of the nations worshipping God,
"every one from his place, even the isles of the heathen"
(2:11) — that is, each race within its own locale and cultural
setting.

The incarnation of the Son of God (Phil. 2:7-8) was within
the social limitations of Judaism, even within a specific lineage
within that nation. With respect to locale, it emerged within a

normal Galilean village structure, within an occupational group in the peasant economy, where Jesus lived as a carpenter and the son of a carpenter (Matt. 13:55; Mark 6:3). His speech also, it would seem, followed the linguistic enclosure of his own people: he probably spoke in the Galilean Aramaic dialect, which was so distinct that it caused comment by the townspeople as near as Jerusalem (Mark 14:70). Jesus himself was known as a countryman and was spoken of as the "prophet of Nazareth" (Matt. 21:10-11). Yet he was sent as the Father's herald to proclaim salvation to all — "whosoever believeth" (John 3:16). Within the social enclosure of Jewish life, language, and custom, Jesus dealt not only with individuals but with kin groups, both he and the Gospel writers recognizing their entity: the Zebedee family (Mark 1:19); Lazarus and his sisters (John 11 and 12); classes of people like the "publicans and sinners" (Luke 15:2; Mark 2:16); village groups, such as those at Cana (John 2:1) and Capernaum (v. 12), drawn together for a festival; occupational groups, like the Bethsaida fishermen (1:44); racial groups (4:40); and huge mixed crowds. He sent his disciples to households and villages (Luke 8:1; 10:5, 8-9, etc.).

The apostles were also alert to *winnable* social segments — they planted household churches (Philem. v. 2, etc.), itinerated through villages (Acts 9:35) and towns (9:42; 10:24, etc.), traveled from district to district and land to land (as, for example, the journeys of Paul). They paid attention to craft groups (18:3), penetrated some intellectual segments (17:32-34), won even magicians in great numbers (19:19) and groups in political employment (Phil. 4:22, in Caesar's household).

Because the Great Commission was expressed in ethnic terms (Matt. 28:19), we look forward to the Great Consummation, when the gospel is to be preached to every "nation, kindred, and tongue" (Rev. 10:11; 14:6). The redeemed will come from all "nations and kindreds and peoples and tongues" (7:9). Only in the new Jerusalem of the messianic age will there be a new and uniform social structure under the King of Kings and Lord of Lords.

In the meantime the Bible does not proclaim that here and now one kind of social structure is ideal. Nor does it proclaim that the English language or idiom shall be the ideal medium for gospel proclamation. The Bible recognizes that all social units are opportunities for the proclamation of the word of God. We ought therefore to be ever aware of the social units about us as groups that are *winnable*. To this end Christ sends us forth into the world (John 17:18). This is his command to us, in the same terms as he had his from the Father.

This is why the church growth method pays considerable attention to the patterns of social units within which people organize themselves for the satisfaction and supply of their human needs, for their problem-solving and their decision-making procedures; that, by their decision for Christ, they may find in him the satisfaction of all their needs and the answers to their problems. It behooves us, as his missionaries, to make ourselves aware of cohesive social segments, and to see these as winnable units within which we may perform our ministry.

GROWTH BY MULTI-INDIVIDUAL DECISION

The basis of church growth is the conversion of individuals; but sometimes the stress we put on the individual obscures the biblical truth that the Holy Spirit also brings men to repentance in groups, families, and tribes. The structure of this movement is *multi-individual,* not mass-movement. The multi-individual structure of the Church is recognized in the familiar, current, collective terminology like "congregation," the "community of God," the "people of God," and the "fellowship." The idea of the congregation goes back to the collective worshipping body of the Psalms and beyond (see 26:12, 68:26), even from the beginning of Israel's history as a nation, where we meet "the assembly of the congregation of Israel" (Exod. 12:6).

The assembly was a public decision-making unit in which the leader made his proclamations, and the people accepted or rejected them. When I read that Moses and Aaron "gathered together all the elders" and "did signs in the sight of the people," and, furthermore, that "the people believed" and "bowed their heads and worshipped" (Exod. 4:29-31), I am convinced that that indicates a multi-individual response rather than a mass one. In any event, the Bible approves it, as it does the corporate worship of the redeemed in the Book of Revelation.

I have heard it argued that our Lord resisted the group concept when he rejected a popular kingship (John 6:15). However, in this incident he was rejecting a wrong concept of Messiahship, not the concept of the group. Furthermore, he was demonstrating that the way of the "popular hero" was not the way of the cross, and for this his time was "not yet come" (John 7:6). We misapply John 6:15 when we use it to argue the Lord's objection to the group per se. Both our Lord and the Bible as a whole show an awareness of the group and the responsibility of the individual within the group.

The Bible shows that the individual has specific responsibility toward his kin (Gen. 4:9). The twelve disciples included a kin unit, brought as inquirers by kin invitation and cohesion (John 1:40-1). In the Old Testament the "people of God" is conceived as a cohesive unit, growing from a nuclear family to an extended family to a lineage. The unit was expected to act cohesively under tribal leaders within the will of God (Deut. 1:13-8). When Israel lost that cohesion and turned to Baalism under the pressure of a foreign queen, God brought them back to himself through dynamic encounter and cohesive multi-individual decision (I Kings 18:37,39).

Biblical phrases like "all with one accord" (Acts 1:13-4; 2:1, 46; 8:5-8) show multi-individual responsibility in group action. Jesus commissioned the seventy in terms of acceptance and rejection by households and villages (Luke 10:5-11), and his postresurrection commission was in terms of tribes or nations (Matt. 28:19). These multi-individual collective concepts indicate that the calling of men by collective action was within the orbit of the purpose of God.

It worked out as he had intended. The disciples received the Spirit as a select group (John 20:22), a loosely held sodality. Likewise, the Spirit came on the twelve men at Ephesus (Acts 19:6-7) and the larger groups at Samaria and at Jerusalem on Pentecost (Acts 2:1-4; 8:14, 17).

Kin unit decisions are more apparent in the Old Testament patriarchal society (which many mission fields of today resemble); but in New Testament Hebraic-Graeco-Roman society (in spite of different decision-making patterns), the cohesive kin unit survived in the substructure — e.g., the sons of Sceva (Acts 19:14). Kin structure, as an instrument through which the Holy Spirit brings people to God (Acts 11:11-18; 16:15), is recognized in household baptism (Acts 16:32-4; I Cor. 1:16). Total communal decision for Christ was recorded at Lydda and Saron (Acts 9:35). The Spirit also moved a large segment of the community at Joppa (Acts 9:42).

Through the history of the Christian Church, the historic action of the Holy Spirit in people-movements out of paganism and revivals within the Church shows the continuing divine approval of church growth by multi-individual decision, at both the discipling and perfecting levels. This should inspire us to pray for further outpourings on kin and village units in our day.

This also permits us to see that new churches may come into being as functioning congregations and may act collectively, even when they are only one step out of paganism. It was so in New Testament times (Acts 8:5-8; 9:35,42); it is so also on the mission field today. These New Testament congregations were multi-individual groups or entities, meeting for the preaching and hearing of the word, for theological instruction, for fellowship, intercessions, and the breaking of bread (2:42). Organic growth was apparent from the start. The twelve recommended the appointment of the seven, with a differentiation of function (6:2-3). This was approved by the congregation, a congregational election took place (v. 5), and the election was followed by an act of ordination (v. 6); and this multi-individual action had God's blessing (v. 7). Later on, under the ministry of Paul, the congregational structure under appointed elders was reinforced. Elders were ordained in every congregation (14:23). Thus were they able to be multi-individual functioning units.

THE CONVERT AND HIS CONTEXT

Church growth theory demands that each convert have an individual experience of salvation, and that he become a new man in Christ; but it does not demand that this must necessarily be identical to any western stereotype. It rather insists that the individual convert must be won for Christ, that he be a new man within his own cultural situation. If he has to be extracted from this context to become a Christian, then he is acculturated rather than converted. On the mission field we have seen this happen all too often. We have seen converts so completely uprooted from their contexts and tradition, so foreignized, that they are left without a home, without a field for social interaction, and sometimes without a means of livelihood. Sometimes these persons have affixed themselves like parasites to a mission station complex and have become so utterly dependent as to be known as "rice-Christians," unrelated to their own world, irrelevant to their relatives, and often regarded as traitors. Church growth research shows that over the years they have tended to become little replicas of western types, poor copies of the missionary, belonging neither to the west nor to their own society.

Church growth theory believes that the Lord wants converts who can live the Christian life within their own social structures — be they industrial, nomadic, or subsistent. We ask the question: what does it mean to be a Christian in this or that kind of society? If our missionary methods extract converts from their society and leave them as social isolates or misfits, there is something wrong with our missioning. I am speaking of normal people, living in normal societies different from ours, not lone outpost individualists, persons isolated by sickness or those called to nomadic apostleship.

This was the very issue debated at the first great conference of the early Church. Did a Gentile have to conform to certain Jewish rites in order to become a Christian? The record of the discussion and the verdict are preserved (Acts 15:1-35). Peter spoke on the basis of his personal experience (vv. 8-11). Paul and Barnabas testified of the work of the Holy Spirit among the Gentiles (v. 12). James made the official pronouncement with admonition (vv. 13-21), after which the decision was circulated by letter and word of mouth (vv. 22-35). This decree, against the forcing of the cultural pattern of the evangelizing people on the evangelized, is written into the foundations of the Church and cries aloud today at the expressly westernizing missionary.

The classic case from the life and ministry of Jesus is the narrative of the Samaritan woman at Sychar (John 4). Jesus did not say to her, as he did to the twelve, "Come, follow me!" He did not say, "You should come out of Sychar and take up residence with my disciples in Jerusalem." There were good reasons against this. In the first place, she would not have been well received in Jerusalem. Even if she had been, she would not have been comfortable; she would not have adapted. In the second place, she belonged to Sychar. Her people were there — the people who needed her help now. If her life was to be changed and elevated, that renewal would have to take place where she was known as the disreputable person she actually was. Furthermore, it was in Sychar that the Master needed her help.

So Jesus let her go back to the place where she belonged, and she became the bridge for his own entry into the place where he himself would never have been received (vv. 29-30, 39). If she was to be a changed woman, she would have to pass the test in Sychar. There she made her testimony, and she introduced Christ to her own group. We often think of this as a case of Jesus dealing with an individual, because he spoke to her of the water of life and revealed to her his Messiahship (v. 26). But at no point did he see her alone as an isolate. She was a key to the group. Inspired, she returned to her context (v. 28), used her experience to introduce others to Christ (vv. 29-30), and by her testimony won some of them to believe (v. 39). Others were won by the word and presence of Jesus himself (vv. 40-1). When Jesus left, two days later, there remained a community of believers. The woman did not have to stand alone; she belonged to a group.

In Mark 5:1-20, we have another enlightening record. A demoniac had been healed. The story tells of the exorcism of the demons. The man was restored to his right mind. It was natural enough for him to desire to remain near the one who had healed him (v. 18), but Jesus did not agree. This man belonged to his own context. He could be of greater use to the Lord by going home; he could be a living testimony of what had been done for him (v. 19). Thus he went around Decapolis, where he was well known, publishing the good news with effect (v. 20).

Although the word of life was explained to Nicodemus (John 3), we have no reason to believe that he fully understood it then. But we note that he too had his context. He was, indeed, so aware of it that he came to Jesus secretly by night (v. 2). Jesus did not let him forget who he was and where he belonged (v. 10). Yet, when we next meet Nicodemus in the Gospel story, he is speaking up for Jesus of his own volition against the critical opposition. Here he was in his true context (John 7:50-52) as a member of the Sanhedrin.

The return of the prodigal son (Luke 15:11-32) is more than a sentimental homecoming. The man belonged to a context even though he had gone away, wasted his substance in riotous living, and disgraced the family name. There was only one way to resolve the situation: by his returning to the place where he belonged and re-establishing himself with those in whose eyes he had failed so dismally. His change of heart had to be demonstrated with all the humiliation it must have involved in the context where he belonged, in the presence of the forgiving father and the unforgiving brother.

If these cases do not cover all the situations we face in the Christian mission, they do at least speak of a good many. The dynamics of religious conversion are so varied that any demand for a stereotyped pattern is dangerous, especially a western pattern. Every conversion has a context of its own, where the regenerated person should testify and demonstrate his changed life. This demonstration should be in terms of the convert's own culture. The convert should ask himself, "How must I live my new life in Sychar, in Decapolis, in the Sanhedrin, in my father's house?" A rice-Christian or a religious isolate does us no credit.

It is significant that Paul began his Christian life testifying to his new-found faith in Christ in the very place where it was known that he had planned persecutions of the Christians (Acts 9:2, 13-4, 20, 22). But Paul was a special case, a chosen vessel, with a wider ministry than this. As a man of wide interests, great education, and a capacity for dialog with philosophers, his context was the Greek world. As we have seen, he had no intention of imposing Jewish cultural standards on his Greek converts, but there was a disputation and a conference before the early Church agreed with him. With the support of Peter the Church was convinced. Peter said, "Why tempt ye God, to put a yoke on the neck of the disciples ...?" (15:10). And James said, "Wherefore my sentence is, that we trouble not them, which from among the Gentiles are turned to God" (v. 19).

For church growth theory, this means that converts should become Christian *within* their own cultures, and should not have a foreign form of Christianity imposed upon them.

ACCEPTANCE AND REJECTION

Most cross-cultural social projects (health, sanitation, education, or agriculture), like the Christian mission itself, are concerned with the major problem of acceptance and rejection. Most advocates of such reforms are firmly convinced that their programs will mean progress and blessing, if accepted by the folk they intend to help. But, alas, how frequently they are rejected. A whole area of research — group dynamics — has been developed about this problem, because a worthy and ideal plan can so easily be obstructed by some overlooked cultural feature.

The theme of acceptance and rejection runs through the Bible. The tragedy and penalty of sin stands over against the alternative of salvation. God's plan of salvation for man is clearly stated, and the Bible reader is never left in doubt about the necessity of making his decision one way or the other, either for the way of life or the way of death. There is no uncommitted middle course.

It was the same with Israel as a people. In that wonderful chapter in which Moses set the alternatives before Israel on the eve of his departure from their midst (Deut. 30), he stated them in terms of life and death, of blessing or curse, and he urged them to *choose* life (v. 19). The concept of the *choice* was pressed again on Israel by Joshua (Josh. 24:14-28). These historic choices were cases of religious decision, collectively demanded in favor of the Lord, against the gods of the land. Furthermore, these choices were legally certified and witnessed (Deut. 30:19; Josh. 24:22, 25-7). Note that in such a tribal society a communal response in unison to the leader's question is the legal procedure for group acceptance of a new position.

The continuity between the lawgivers and the prophets is significant. When Israel's religion was in danger from foreign worship, and Elijah felt he stood alone against 450 prophets of Baal in that dramatic power encounter on Mount Carmel (I Kings 18:22), the people again registered their decision in a group demonstration by falling on their faces and declaring their choice for the Lord against the worship of Baal (v. 39).

With the emergence of the individualism of the prophets of the Babylonian period and the need for personal (as distinct from communal) commitment, the same continuity is revealed. God still demanded a decision from man (Jer. 21:8).

Jesus took his stand on the prophetic tradition of Israel. In both his public preaching and private presentations, he never lost sight of the real purpose of his leading individuals and groups to their respective points of decision (John 4:13-4, 39-42). He longed for acceptance and grieved over rejection (Matt. 19:22-4; Mark 10:21-3; John 6:64, etc.). He was aware of the human factors which hinder acceptance (John 4:43-4; Matt. 19:22-4). He distinguished between the straight and narrow way and the broad way (Matt. 7:13-4), between the food which perisheth and that which is eternal (John 6:27), and between the things of the flesh and those of the Spirit (John 6:62-63). In all these passages we are confronted with decision-making mechanisms.

Not only by Jesus' own example, but also by his words to the apostles, the Christian is pressed into service as an advocate seeking acceptance of his message (Matt. 28:19-20). Christ even went so far as to tell the apostles not to waste their time in a locality where they met with rejection, but to go on to another locality (Luke 9:5), a practice carried out literally in the apostolic Church (Acts 13:51).

Throughout apostolic preaching there was a continual appeal for acceptance of the gospel (Acts 2:38; 3:26; 16:31, etc.). Furthermore, the ultimate gathering of the redeemed "from every nation and tribe and people and language" (Rev. 7) before the Lamb will be an assembly of acceptors of the message of salvation, and they will declare this conviction in their song (v. 10). No other book of the Bible distinguishes more clearly the final state of acceptors from rejectors.

Therefore, the priority that claims our attention as a Church and as Christians is to declare the gospel vocally for acceptance (Acts 10:42-43; 15:3, 12; II Cor. 6:2) and warn of the consequences of rejection (13:32, 38-41). The Holy Spirit blesses the human advocate and works in the heart of the acceptor. The plan of salvation is of the Lord, but he needs a human advocate to proclaim it (Acts 26:17-20; Rom. 10:13-15).

All our social projects should be seen as applications of the faith, as essential outworkings of this acceptance, but certainly not as substitutes for it. When a mission becomes a mere demonstration of our supposed virtue in service projects, it is a form of self-righteousness which obstructs real gospel proclamation. It is humanistic in that it directs the observer to man instead of to God, to the good works which we can do instead of to the salvation which we as men cannot effect. We cannot offer a service demonstration as a substitute for gospel proclamation. The Greek word for "proclaim" implies the role of a herald announcing something with the authority of his lord, and it does not allow for the idea that the proclamation could depend on the ability or virtue of the herald. While it is true that we should be worthy heralds of the Lord whom we represent, salvation depends on *who* has originated the proclamation and what he has proclaimed rather than the messenger. Our message comes from the Lord and concerns an offer of life which men must accept or reject. However, if we heralds do not live lives worthy of our calling, we will certainly hinder the advocacy of the gospel, and this may cause men to reject it. Whereas the gospel stands above the person of the herald, the herald is to present it in such a way as to gain a positive verdict of acceptance.

The New Testament proclamation doctrine is in line with the corpus of witness-bearing material that purports to come from the Lord himself. The apostles were called to a program of witness (John 15:26-7), even though they would be persecuted for doing so (16:1-4). In I John 1, the apostle declares the witness-bearing program (v. 2) and its purpose of incorporating acceptors into the fellowship (v. 3). Paul also had received word from the Lord through Ananias to witness for decision (Acts 22:15), and again in a vision he was assured he would bear witness at Rome (23:11).

There seems to me to be no escape from the position that the apostle is appointed an advocate to proclaim Jesus Christ and the gospel for acceptance. This is a call that involves a power encounter. The Christian is involved not merely in the resistance of evil (Eph. 6:12), but in a definite turning from idols to God—a positive demonstration of acceptance (I Thess. 1:9). The concept of the decision-making choice and its need for continual proclamation is essential in biblical Christianity.

We have a considerable corpus of scriptural material demonstrating the unity of the Bible in this respect. The concept runs through the Psalms and Prophets, through the teaching of Jesus and the apostles. There is, for example, the idea of Christ as the Rock or Stone. The psalmist (118:21-24), Isaiah the prophet (8:13-15), Jesus himself (Luke 20:17-18), and the apostle Peter (Acts 4:11-12; I Pet. 2:6-8) all use the metaphor. The subject in each case is acceptance or rejection of Christ. On the one hand we have acceptance, believing, salvation, and incorporation. On the other hand rejection means offense, stumbling, judgment, and isolation. It was Jesus who took this Old Testament idea and certified that it should be applied to him. Peter, as a faithful advocate, proclaimed it at the beginning and the end of his ministry.

It seems to me that the Bible says that the advocate (the preacher) is obliged to proclaim Christ for acceptance and warn against rejecting him.

FUNCTIONAL ROLES AND INGATHERING

A critic says, "We are not commanded to be fruitful, but to be faithful." I object to this distinction between "fruitful" and "faithful." Scripturally, "faithful" has several meanings, and one of them is "fruitful" — faithful in achieving expected results. Examples of this use are in the parables of the talents (Matt. 25:21,23), the pounds (Luke 19:17), the steward responsible for supplying meat (Matt. 24:45; Luke 12:42). Achieved results are evidence of faith, in line with James 2:17-18, 20-22 and Philippians 3:14. There is a whole corpus of material — in terms of stewardship, building, etc. — indicating faithfulness by results. The builder who fails to accomplish his role is ridiculed (Luke 14:30). What owner would say to his steward, Never mind results? Builders and stewards are appointed to get results.

The concept of stewardship is well developed. Two Greek words are used: a house manager, who sees that the servants do their work (Luke 12:42; 16:1ff.); and an overseer, tutor, or agent (Matt. 20:8), whose job is to communicate effectively and get results. Stewardship is a functional role expectant of results, and the steward comes under judgment of his lord (25:21,23,26; Luke 16:2; 19:17,22ff.; I Cor. 4:1-4), especially if he resigns himself to an expectancy of no return by burying his talent in the earth.

Another functional role conceptualized by Jesus was that of the husbandman, appointed to care for the vineyard in order that it might produce more fruit. This person was expected to supervise labor and arrange the harvesting program. The landowner relied on him. Jesus "thrust" this concept at the chief priests and Pharisees, seeing them as unprofitable husbandmen in another parable of judgment (Matt. 21:33-45; Mark 12:1-9; Luke 20:9-19). James also used the idea of the functional role of the husbandman (5:7). In a similar role, the dresser of the vineyard was told to grub the fruitless tree (Luke 13:6-9).

The farmer, whether sower or harvester, has a functional role whose object is the harvest in due season. The sower knows he depends on God for seed, sun, and rain; but he cultivates expecting that his work, under God, will produce a good return (Matt. 13:8; Mark 4:8; Luke 8:8).

Jesus also spoke in spiritual terms of the functional role of those he called from the fishercraft, that they become fishers of men (Matt. 4:18-22; Mark 1:16-20; Luke 5:10-11). The significant part of this imagery to Peter is manifest in his behavior — his counting of the number of fish taken (John 21:11).

These allegories of responsibility and expectation of results come from one strand of Jesus' ministry: the calling and training of the twelve. He called them and trained them in this functional task of ingathering — cultivating for the harvest, stewardship for fruit, fishing for a catch — and assured them they would be held responsible.

This theory of the training of the apostles was demonstrated by the Master symbolically at the beginning (Luke 5) and the end (John 21) of his ministry and also in the harvest at Sychar (John 4:35-36, 39-42). The last occasion was also an actual demonstration of intake accompanied by the metaphor. For their own practical work, he sent them out on a student mission (Luke 10:1-24), and, when his mission and message had been totally put before them, he commissioned them to the functional ministry of ingathering (Matt. 28:18-20).

This all speaks to us in the Christian mission. As stewards we are to work for and to expect a return. If our crops do not reach our expectations we ought to examine our work, applying all the knowledge and techniques at our disposal as stewards. If need be, trees have to be pruned. It may be that, if a tree is barren, it needs removal altogether, that the ground be used for something more productive. True, the rain, the sun, the seed, and the growth itself are all of the Lord alone; but we are the cultivators, and he has appointed us. We are called and trained for a functional role, and we must apply our technical knowledge to the expectant end of ingathering. Inasmuch as bad methods, failure to prune, to irrigate, to manure, to plow, and to weed fall under the functional role of steward, such an official must be held responsible for growth or non-growth.

It therefore behooves us to continually examine our methods in conjunction with our actual ingathering. It is right that we "judge ourselves that we be not judged" of the Lord; for, as he said to the Church at Thyatira, "I will give unto every one of you according to his works" (Rev. 2:23).

THE NONCULTURAL FACTOR

Whereas the church growth viewpoint urges field missionaries and mission policy-makers to pay attention to cultural factors that can stimulate or obstruct growth, we must never forget that certain noncultural factors are operative in every situation. Some of these cannot be measured, although the manifestation of their activity may be observed. The most significant of these is the divine factor, spoken of either as the work of God himself, or of the Holy Spirit.

He who creates the seed, sends the rain, causes the sun to shine, and determines the precise moment at which the harvest turns yellow to ripeness is the major actor in the drama, even though he uses sowers, cultivators, and reapers to help him. It is true that good cultivation and correct harvesting do have some bearing on the quantitative and qualitative aspects of the ingathering, but these do not produce the growth itself. Old and New Testament alike speak of God as Creator (Eccl. 12:1; Isa. 40:28; 43:15; Rom. 1:25; I Pet. 4:19, etc.), and reveal him as the one who provides the basic needs of man (Psa. 23:1; Phil. 4:19, etc.). The Bible shows the mind of the Creator, who pronounced his handiwork good (Gen. 1:4,10,12,18,21,25), that the earth should be fruitful (v. 11) and that man should cultivate it to productivity (2:15).

Social anthropologists have observed that it takes more than just setting up a structure of helpful factors to persuade a society to accept a major social change. Change will not be accepted, says Kroeber, until the culture permits. He cites the genius who had discovered a great truth, only to find it rejected by the people for forty years because the time was not ripe. The full explanation, however, is not as simple as Kroeber would have his readers believe, although he does emphasize an important fact — that there are times of ripeness and of unripeness. Thus, a good idea or innovation may well be rejected at a certain time. This matter is dealt with in the section, "Acceptance and Rejection." Meanwhile, the reference is of some value to us in our present discussion, because the imagery of the harvest is prominent. We are confronted in the Bible with fields ripening at different times. A small part of Samaria, for instance, a unit at Sychar, was ripe when Jesus visited the place (John 4:35). Another part of the same country did not ripen to harvest until the days of Philip (Acts 8:5-8) and Peter (v. 25). A noncultural factor was operative here. It is in the providence of God, and fortunate for the farmer, that all the fields in one locality do not ripen precisely at the same time, but their ripening is distributed over the harvest season.

Even the Lord himself was under the limitations of time. So he spoke of his time being "not yet come" (John 2:4; 7:8). Indeed, in John's Gospel we frequently meet this mode of speech — his (or her) "hour" (7:30; 8:20; 13:1; 16:21) or "the hour is come" (17:1). All of this indicates a divine will behind the drama. Furthermore, the incarnation of our Lord was set in time as God saw it, when "the fullness of the time was come" (Gal. 4:4). In the same phrase we are told that all things will be gathered together to the cosmic Christ (Eph. 1:10). His death for sinners also was "in due time" (Rom. 5:6). This is the biblical view of God in history.

In the dynamism of the early Church, the divine activity is seen as an outpouring of his Spirit (Acts 2:17-18; 10:45). The Holy Spirit is the initiator of mission (13:2-4). Paul was constrained to change his program in Asia because of the intervention of the Spirit (16:6); and Philip had a similar experience when taken from an active people-movement in Samaria for another special mission (8:5-8,29). The experience of conversion, although we can explain the process in terms of psychological abstractions, still leaves some aspects which defy explanation. We say that the Holy Spirit is at work, and this is still the most satisfactory explanation. Certain phenomena that frequently accompany conversion and are attributed to the Spirit (2:4; 10:44-46) cannot be explained in cultural terms. Many of us have seen things happen on the mission field for which neither cultural nor scientific explanations can be found. The Bible attributes these things to the work of the Holy Spirit or to some other spirit (e.g., 19:14-16).

Anthropology can often show us how a Christward people-movement works along well-known lines of social structure and cultural communication, but it cannot explain the spiritual enthusiasm per se. It cannot explain the dramatic moral change in conversion or the spiritual victory after a dynamic encounter with an evil power. It can objectively record these things as facts and detect social influences here and there, but the basic change of life still defies anthropological explanation. How does one account for the ability of Philip and Peter to turn "many villages of the Samaritans," and both bewitched persons and their bewitcher to the gospel of the Nazarene (Acts 8:5-25)? This calls for a clever explanation from both psychologist and anthropologist. The Bible ascribes this kind of work to the Holy Spirit. It is up to the skeptics to explain away this frame of reference and to produce a more tenable system of explanation. Science records that men have become "new creatures." It may explain the psychological process of the conversion experience and demonstrate that the behavioral patterns tend to be culturally conditioned and can be identified and classified, but the noncultural factor still remains. The vital question is still unanswered: what really changes the bad man into a good man, what changes his mental set, and how does he know "the grace wherein he stands"?

If salvation is for "whosoever believeth," we do not wonder that the Holy Spirit should work through the cultural structures within which men live and express themselves and satisfy their needs. The God who is at work in human history is also at work in human society. Within many different patterns, men are being made new creatures. If some elements of that process are beyond our human comprehension, that does not mean they are not true. In church growth studies, then, we are examining the cultural matrix within which God has chosen to work. An honest researcher can never eliminate the divine element from his analysis.

Having said this, I must add a warning. The fact that God has the harvest in his hands does not relieve man of his obligation to be faithful in his role in the partnership. Both the quantity and the quality of the harvest are influenced to some extent by the cultivator and harvester, for God has so ordained it. He depends on us.

The human responsibility lies also in the recognition of the fact that the field is ready for harvest:

> Say not ye, There are yet four months and then cometh the harvest? Behold I say unto you, Lift up your eyes, and look on the fields; for they are ripe already to harvest. (John 4:35)

This truth has bearing on the whole question of strategic deployment of personnel and funds in missions. Some day we shall have to give our report to the Lord of the harvest. As

Paul pointed out to the Corinthians, "Now is the accepted time, now is the day of salvation" (II Cor. 6:2). The harvest has to be recognized as ripe, and the harvesters must be sent at once. The ripened grain in the allegory indicates the work of the Holy Spirit. On this point John Wesley used a different metaphor:

> This is the time when we should second the motions of the blessed Spirit. . . .
> Providence and the Spirit of God go before and open up the way. (Sermon on "The Means of Grace")

Church growth method therefore recognizes the operation of noncultural (or divine) factors in bringing situations to a ripeness for decision. The most important of these is the Holy Spirit's work of prevenient grace. Our missionary responsibility is to be alert to opportunity when God, in his goodness, sets it before us.

III

Problems of Non-Growth

There is a verse in the Old Testament that suggests the title for this section. A battle had been won; the terms had been agreed to. But nothing had been done about carrying out those terms. "Know ye not that Ramoth in Gilead is ours, and we be still, and take it not...?" (I Kings 22:3). It was an *unpossessed* possession. The Bible recognizes the fact that many of the rightful possessions of the people of God still have to be possessed. It is possible for something to be ours and yet not ours.

Take the idea of "possessing the promised land" that runs through the Book of Deuteronomy — it is mentioned more than fifty times. It was to this end that they came out of Egypt (Exod. 3:7-8), and the possession of Canaan was a divine promise (Deut. 30:5, etc.). Promised also was the moral equipment for the task of entry (4:5; 6:1; 11:8, etc.). The promises had been reiterated at Horeb (1:8), at Kadesh-Barnea (1:21), in the Valley of Beth-peor (4:1), at Pisgah (6:18; 8:1), and at the end of the Song of Moses, where the promise was transmitted to the next generation under Joshua (32:45-7). All that remained was to cross over the river and possess the land (9:1-4; 11:31). Yet how long had they remained in that wilderness? It was always that God was promising them the land, reassuring them that this was his will; but it would never be really theirs until they were moved to action, to go forth in obedience to possess it (15:5; 30:15-20).

Is it not the same with our salvation? The battle has been won on the cross; the promise has been made (I John 1:9;

John 3:16). He is able to save to the uttermost (Heb. 7:25).
Whom? All who come to God by him. He died for our sin and
was raised for our justification (Rom. 4:25); but, although this
new life is ours, yet it is not ours unless we possess it: "It is of
faith, that it might be by grace; to the end that the promise
might be sure." One has to accept his possession. Thus, said
Wesley:

> Bold I approach the eternal throne,
> And claim the crown, through Christ, my own.

The land is not possessed by wandering in the wilderness;
Jordan must be crossed. Salvation is not achieved by understanding a doctrine intellectually; an acceptance and experience of possession is required.

This is also the case in the Christian mission. When we
plant, cultivate, and weed the field of the Lord, we expect
an ingathering — otherwise, toward what goal do we labor?
In his time God turns the green crop yellow to harvest. This
harvest he gives, but ours is the task of the ingathering. The
field is still the world, so much of which is ripe to harvest in
our day. The Church must possess her harvest, but the harvesters are all too few. We have received specific word from
the Lord in this very imagery of the harvest — when he sent
the seventy out into their own known locality for an ingathering (Luke 10:2).

The harvest is not the only figure of this kind. We have, for
instance, the vintage and the catch of fish. Their common de-
nominator is that they are all potentials, promises given by a
providential God, but remaining unrealized, unpossessed possessions, until the harvesters, vinedressers, or fishermen have
gathered in their harvest.

One of the fine concepts in the Old Testament, taken over
by the New, is the notion of inheritance. The Old Testament
contains over four hundred references to inheritance. In the
New Testament we meet it in these forms: "inheriting the
promises" (Heb. 6:12), "inheriting blessing" (I Pet. 3:9), "inheriting the kingdom of God" (I Cor. 6:9-10; 15:50; Gal. 5:21),
"inheriting the kingdom prepared for you" (Matt. 25:34) and
"inheriting eternal life" (Matt. 19:29; Mark 10:17; Luke
10:25; 18:18). Clearly, then, it is the will of God for his chil-

dren to become "partakers of the inheritance of the saints" (Col. 1:12).

This last Pauline reference goes on to show that the kingdom and redemption are ours through Christ (vv. 13-14), but we are committed to a ministry of preaching, warning, and teaching, that men may possess their possessions and become "mature in Christ" (v. 28). To this missionary goal the apostle strives (v. 29). It seem to me that this implies Paul's awareness of the tragic possibility that some may not possess this promised inheritance, because, either (1) they have deliberately rejected it, or (2) the preacher has not presented it with sufficient urgency.

A harvest left too long unreaped will rot in the field. The day of opportunity passes, as Jeremiah bemoaned in his prophetic dirge:

> Why have they provoked me to anger with graven images
>   and with their foreign idols?
> The harvest is past, the summer is ended,
>   and we are not saved.
>
> (Jer. 8:19-20. Cf. Joel 1:10-2)

Because of lost opportunities, Jesus wept over Jerusalem:

> How often would I have gathered thy children together ... and ye would not! Behold your house is left unto you desolate.... (Luke 13:34-5)

It is because of this tragic possibility, the possibility in our day that men for whom Christ died may yet be lost, that the Christian mission is still an urgent necessity. After Jesus had died on the cross and risen with power, he sent his followers forth to the ends of the earth, that men everywhere might hear and possess what was now theirs. This commission has never been completed or revoked. His own mission on earth was to seek and save the lost (Luke 19:10). He transmitted this task to his followers (John 20:21) in the terms of his own mission and gave them the Holy Spirit to help them perform this role (v. 22).

We cannot escape the fact that the Bible recognizes the lostness of man unless he possesses his possessions. In the visions of the last days, the angel of God calls his people in the cry against Babylon: "Come out of her, my people, that ye be not partakers of her sins, and that ye receive not her plagues"

(Rev. 18:4). We can feel strongly the tragedy of the lostness of man.

We live in a day when millions of animistic people are changing their religion. The Church is called not merely to a Christian presence, but to a specific, positive mission of winning the nations *(panta ta ethnē)*. To pass from the commission (Matt. 28:19) to the consummation, it is in the power of the slain Lamb (Rev. 5:6) that the "seven Spirits of God," the churches, are "sent forth unto all the earth," and, in this victory of his, that the song of redemption is to be sung by the redeemed "out of every kindred and tongue and people and nation" (v. 9). This international and intertribal worshipping community (7:9-17) in the vision of the consummation lies before us as a possession to be possessed.

Furthermore, the Great Consummation is cast in terms of the Church, as the bride of Christ, and the marriage supper of the Lamb (19:7-9). The faithful are to be gathered there. But, set over against this picture is another of the tragedy of the lost (20:15, etc.). If we accept the Bible as our rule for faith and action, we cannot escape this fact.

The responsibility for mission is stated at the very end of the book in terms of invitation, as much as to say that this is the last word of God about the plight of man, for no man is to add to this word (22:18). "The Spirit and the Bride say 'Come!' Let him that heareth say 'Come!' " The Bride or the Church is involved in invitation to the end. So too is the convert. The water of life is free, but he who is thirsty must come and drink — i.e., to possess his possession (22:17). To the very end of the Bible, we are confronted with the gospel invitation and the divine desire for man's acceptance.

OBSTRUCTING THE WORK OF GOD

From the tragic possibility of unpossessed possessions, we pass to the equally tragic possibility of the actual obstruction of God's work by his human agents.

Some people start from the presupposition that, as God is sovereign, "whatever will be will be" (as the popular song puts it); and that as long as we exist merely as a Christian presence in the world, we can leave the rest to him. This is surely to confuse the *immediate* and *ultimate,* and to overlook our responsibility as his servants. Of course, the ultimate end lies with God, but in the meantime we may either help or hinder his immediate purpose. The work of God here and now in this world can certainly be obstructed by our attitudes. If this is not so, a great deal of instruction in Scripture has no point.

Let us consider for a moment the imagery of burning, the symbolism of which has been used in several ways in Scripture. The frequent recurrence of the phrase "fire which shall not be quenched" as a symbol of the finality and totality of judgment in both the Old and New Testaments reminds us that a fire may be maintained or quenched, may burn or die. Sometimes in Scripture the emphasis is on the importance of maintaining the burning light and the danger of the fire being quenched. In this connection, burning may be used as the symbol of our faith and service. Incense, as a symbol of prayer, and burning light may symbolize God's presence. There are many examples of this burning in both the Old Testament (e.g., II Chron. 13:10-2) and the New Testament (cf. Rev. 4:5; 8:3-4; Luke 1:10). It was the symbol of the prophet's call in the burning bush (Exod. 3:2) and of purification for Isaiah (Isa. 6:6). Our Lord himself used the symbolism of the burning lamp (Matt. 5:15; 25:1-10; Luke 8:16), and later on lamps were the symbol of the Christian churches witnessing in the world (Rev. 1:12, etc.).

There are two distinctive features of the symbolism of burning in the New Testament:

(1) The burning fire is the symbol of the Spirit of God within the world and in the life of man. When the risen Lord expounded the Scriptures to the disciples on the way to Emmaus, he introduced them to the experience of the burning heart (Luke 24:32). Tongues of fire were also the symbol of the Pentecostal experience (Acts 2:3).

(2) The individual disciple and the community of disciples (the Church) are called to be lamps and, as lamps, are responsible for lighting the darkness by burning (Matt. 5:14-16).

The thing so frequently overlooked is the tragic possibility of that burning's being quenched. Whether we see this burning as the work of the Spirit in our midst or our own role of burning in the Evangel and in Christian service, the burning must be maintained. We are responsible.

The parable of the wise and foolish virgins (Matt. 25:1-13) brings this out perfectly. In contrast to the concept of responsibility (servicing the lamps and being ready when the moment of action comes), our Lord set the picture of irresponsibility (failure to service the lamps and unreadiness); the one ended in reception into, and the other exclusion from the marriage feast — fellowship or judgment.

The same possibility of rejection under the symbol of the extinguished lamp is seen in the warning given to the Ephesian Church (Rev. 2:5). Thus, the biblical figure distinguishes between the *immediate* and the *ultimate*. The immediate work of the Spirit can be hindered by us, and we are thus exposed to judgment. We do not realize the danger until we first see the terrible possibility of God's work in our time and place actually being obstructed by our attitudes.

Thus Paul warns the Thessalonians, "Quench not the Spirit" (I Thess. 5:19), and he exhorts the Ephesians to "grieve not the Holy Spirit" (4:30). He said the same thing in other ways at other places. For instance, he urged the Corinthians to suffer all things "lest we should hinder the gospel of Christ" (I Cor. 9:12). Nor is the idea confined to the New Testament. The psalmist, considering the rebellious children of Israel in the wilderness, saw them as holding up the Lord's program and said, "They limited the Holy One of Israel" (Psa. 78:41).

Let us not resign ourselves to the inevitability of "whatever will be will be," but let us remember that we are involved in the Lord's program, and by our attitudes we may hasten or hinder the day of the Lord. At this point it becomes incumbent on those of us responsible for missionary programming to examine our purposes and methods continually — the servicing of the lamps committed to our care. This is a basic presupposition of all church growth research, so that our shortcomings may not hinder the burning.

THE PRINCIPLE OF STRATEGIC LOCATION

Strategic location of missionary effort and employment of

resources stand on the law of acceptance and rejection. John stated it in the prologue to his Gospel (1:11-12): some reject, others accept. Adoption into the family of God is by accept-ance.

The Lord stated the principle in his instructions to the seventy (Luke 10:5-6, 8-11), where the imagery is in the familiar terms of harvest (v. 2), and the teaching purpose is to show judgment on a basis of acceptance or rejection. The re-jection of the Lord's emissaries calls for a clear-cut counter-rejection of the rejectors, stated in severe terms (vv. 10-11), and followed by a biblical "woe" (v. 13).

Jesus saw Israel's mission in terms of acceptance, rejection, and judgment. In the parable of the vineyard (Matt. 21:37-38), he submitted the parable to the audience for solution. They recommended a change of strategy (v. 41). Jesus interpreted the parable: the inheritance of unfaithful Israel would be given to the nation bringing forth fruit (v. 43). The concept of Israel as the *chosen* people does not imply a certain divine favoritism, as some seem to think, but an opportunity of grace, a calling that involved the assumption of the servant role among the nations (Isa. 43:10). It was the fact that they had interpreted themselves as special objects of God's favor and rejected the servant role that led to their own rejection (Matt. 21:43). In the parable of the marriage feast (Matt. 22:2-10), the invited guests rejected an invitation to joyous fellowship. Therefore the invitation was given to another group — those people in the highways and hedges (8-9).

The Lord's own experience confirmed this. Except for a few persons, his work was with Israel. The early superficial accept-ance of Jesus by the crowd later turned to rejection. Only a small band remained. The official rejection came in the Jewish trial and the Jewish influence in the Roman trial. After the resurrection, the Lord's instructions to the apostles had a new note: Go to *all* nations (Matt. 28:19; Luke 24:47), or into *all* the world (Mark 16:15). The new criterion was "them that believe" (Mark 16:16-17). The apostles were commissioned to ingathering, the symbol of which is baptism (Matt. 28:19; Mark 16:16). Israel had had her opportunity; the offer was thenceforth extended to those "who will believe." The program expanded from Jerusalem in concentric circles, through Judea and Samaria, to the uttermost parts (Acts 1:8). Israel was not completely abandoned, but she had to meet the requirement of acceptance — and still does.

A Jewish branch of Christianity remained, but most Jews rejected the gospel. At Pisidian Antioch, Paul was confronted with both rejecting and accepting groups (Acts 13:42ff.). He turned from the Jews to Gentiles, and the Church grew (vv. 48-49). In Corinth, where Paul had already won some Jews and Greeks (18:1-4), he made another effort to win Jews (v. 5), but his effort failed. He rejected them as a group (v. 6); only a few individuals received the gospel and worshipped with the Greeks. Paul was always ready to speak to a group of elders or in a synagogue, that some should believe. At Rome, some did believe (28:23); but to those who rejected the gospel he made a dramatic pronouncement in terms of prophecy (vv. 25-29), that the gospel they had rejected would be offered to Gentiles, because "they will hear it" (v. 28).

On each of these occasions the criterion was readiness to hear, or willingness to accept the gospel. Having found more willingness among Gentiles than among Jews, Paul turned from the closed to the open doors.

Although the apostle will minister in all places, he is obliged to husband his time and effort and turn to the open doors, "that the wedding may be furnished with guests" (Matt. 22:10). Paul would stay in any responding locality; but, if doors were locked against him in a locality, he would not stay there knocking unduly long. His criterion was readiness to believe. He sought people who would respond, and there he planted churches. This method of mission work supported what Jesus told the seventy.

SERVICE AND MISSION

If the last study gives us a clear biblical directive about deployment, it also raises a problem. For example, what do we do in a resistant country where there is perhaps a law against evangelism and where Christians are tolerated only for the sake of their medical, agricultural, or educational services?

There is a small corpus of teaching in the gospel that has

something to say about this type of situation. However, before we turn to examine it, we need to clarify a point about which there is considerable confusion in the church today. We are not dealing here with the Christian mission at all. This is a service project, pure and simple. We help the sick, we teach the ignorant, and do good to all men. This is our Christian duty. We do it because of the need of fellow men, both at home and abroad; it is a valid claim on the resources of the Church. Church growth theory recognizes this as part of the maturity or perfecting of the Church, and there is no argument at this point.

However, although the Bible recognizes the Church's responsibility for service, it does not confuse *service* and *mission;* for mission is, by definition, a witness with an appeal for verdict, a process of "making disciples."

The Bible recognizes the differentiation of functions in both work and role within the Church. The early Church assigned and/or approved the appointment of persons to types of specialization (Rom. 12:4-8; Eph. 4:11; I Cor. 12:4-30). Because there was confusion about service and mission, specialization was deliberately introduced into the early Church. A group of devoted and intelligent persons was set aside to specialize in service (Acts 6:2-3), so that the preaching of the word (v. 3) would not be disturbed. This was not to say that the deacon could not preach, and that the evangelist was not expected to serve with good works; but each was designated to a specific emphasis, that the Church's ministry might be a total one. The Church is responsible for finding resources in money and men to engage in a total outreach: service to mankind without any expectation of return, and mission, a strategic placement of resources to bring the best possible return for the kingdom of God. One is the role of the servant, the other the role of the steward and apostle.

The confusion arises when some missionary promoters define *service* as *mission* and allow it to stand alone as a substitute for mission, robbing the latter of its demand for a verdict. The biblical view is that the Church's outreach needs both service and mission. The idea that service per se is mission, even when there is no appeal for a verdict, is not biblical and is resisted by the church growth viewpoint.

In church growth theory we say that, if the Church serves an unresponsive community with no expectation of growth and no appeal for decision, and if it recognizes that this is purely a service of love from the "haves" to the "have-nots," this is an honorable service. But if that service agency designates this mere Christian presence as mission and uses the missionary resources in men and money to this end, when a nearby field is ripe to harvest and the laborers are few, this is bad strategy and bad stewardship. Church growth recognizes the service project as Christian duty and a manifestation of perfection growth (maturity). What it opposes is the service project's being publicized as mission and drawing mission resources, since it is no substitute for mission in that it strives for no gospel acceptance. When it robs the true mission of its resources, it falls under the criteria for judging mission that are laid down by our Lord and explained in the last chapter.

In the light of that clarification of the situation, let us now look at the service project in a country where mission is forbidden. Seeing that there is no likelihood of ingathering, such imagery as harvesting and catching fish offers us no solution. The field is just not ripe for reaping. However, perhaps some help may be found in a small corpus of New Testament teaching on the subject of "watching." Certain incidents and parables suggest that sometimes the Christian has to watch and wait.

There was that dark hour in the Lord's period of deep trial when he asked his selected followers to watch. They failed him badly and thereby grieved him (Matt. 26:36-45; Mark 14:32-42). In both these accounts and again in Luke (21:36) and Mark (13:35), Jesus urged the disciples to "watch and pray." The occasions were different, but there was a common didactic element: they were to be ready for something which might come upon them suddenly. They were called to a continuous vigil of watching and praying.

Does not this have meaning for the personnel in Christian service in a country where evangelism is forbidden with the threat of expulsion? Should it be that at least a small force should be retained, watching and praying while they serve, ready to alert the Church at large upon the first signs of any changed attitudes or opportunities for mission? This would certainly fall in line with the Lord's parable of the wise and foolish virgins (Matt. 25:1-13), where we again are injoined to "watch and pray" (v. 13).

Yet, to be exegetically fair, one should point out that these are actually warnings to Christian disciples against temptation in connection with their awaiting the return of the Lord. When we apply them to our present subject, as I have suggested, we are using them allegorically. All we can really say is that this concept of waiting for the Lord's return *seems* to say something to Christians in a resistant country, awaiting an open door for mission. When it comes, it may come without warning. If we are watching and praying, we shall be ready for it when it comes.

In any case, we should be honest with ourselves. Christians are "created in Christ Jesus unto good works" (Eph. 2:10), and directed "with good will doing service, as to the Lord" (Eph. 6:7). "Works and charity and service" (Rev. 2:19) are expected both from the Church as a corporate body or congregation and from the individual Christians (Acts 9:36).

What comes out of our discussion is that social service is service rendered to men as unto the *Lord*. This is a legitimate claim on the resources of the Church, but when it devours the resources designated for mission, it falls under the judgment of mission, as set forth in the scriptural law of deployment.

This does not mean that a service project cannot engage in effective mission, or vice versa. Stephen was a deacon and also an evangelist; but he was an evangelist, not because of his service, but because his service was supported by a communicated message for a verdict.

IV

Church Growth and the Current Situation

One of the unscriptural twists of contemporary theology, which both harms church growth theory and hinders the actual growth of the church, is the idea of a "churchless ministry," the adequacy of merely "being a Christian out there in the world" without the need for a specific worshipping fellowship.

It seems to me that this is a plain rejection of Scripture. The idea of the congregation runs through the Old Testament. It was in this community and social pattern that God elected to bring forth his Son and in which our Lord chose to worship and work (Luke 4:16).

When he established the work that was to be left in the hands of his disciples, our Lord modified the Hebrew concept of the congregation to fit the requirements of the Christian gospel for repentance and response. Instead of being a congregation into which people were born, it became one into which they were *incorporated*.

His intention was quite clear in the Gospels. He called into being a band of disciples around himself as Master (Luke 6:13), as a flock about a shepherd (John 10:2-5). He spoke of *"my* Church" (Matt. 16:18). These are corporate figures of speech with the following configuration:

(1) Christ is central.
(2) He invites or calls men to him.
(3) Those who hear him respond by coming.
(4) Separated as persons from their families (Luke 14:25-27, 33) or an entity distinguished as a flock (John 10:26-28)

from the world, they are incorporated into a fraternity
of disciples. Though from different folds, they form one
flock around the Lord himself (John 10:16). He speaks;
they know him and are known by him (10:14).

The achievement and preservation of the totality of the
group meant a great deal to Jesus (Luke 15:3-7, John 10:29).
To the "little flock" (Luke 12:32) the incorporation represents
a spiritual entity and sense of belonging — which is the very
thing a lonely individual in the crowd craves most of all.
Loneliness is the psychological basis of half the world's ills.

It was to this end that Jesus gave the command to baptize
(Matt. 28:19). We argue much about how and when to baptize
and miss the main point — that this is the symbol of *incorporation*. When Jesus said, "Go, make disciples," he did not
leave it there; disciples also have to be incorporated into the
fellowship of discipleship. The Lord's Supper also is a corporate rite, with Jesus as the center of the group (Luke 22:14ff.).

Christ's concept was pressed by the apostles in like manner.
John's great passage (I John 1:1-4) shows the sequence: his
personal testimony, the invitation that men might believe (vv.
1-2), and the result that those who respond are incorporated
into the fellowship (v. 3), that their joy might be full (v. 4).
Here again is entity and a sense of belonging.

The apostle Paul, apart from using the word church(es)
over sixty times, supplied several corporate figures of speech to
develop this same doctrine. He rejoiced that his converts were
no longer "strangers and foreigners" but "fellow citizens" and
members of the household of God (Eph. 2:19). Then, changing the metaphor, he saw them as part of a building under
construction, "growing into a holy temple in the Lord,"
"builded together" (vv. 21-22). The imagery is that of the
process of growth by incorporation into a total structure.

The metaphor of the spiritual house is used also by Peter
(I Pet. 2:5), and in that same chapter we have other collective
figures of speech: the "royal priesthood" (an organized community sacrificing and mediating), the "holy nation," and
"peculiar people" (v. 9). All these symbols of the corporate
group suggest that the Church does not exist as an end in itself but has its responsible ministry and mission in the world.

In Acts, the Church appears as a worshipping, witnessing, and growing body (Acts 2:46-47), a body meeting for instruction, fellowship, the breaking of bread, and prayers (v. 42). In the letters to the seven churches in Asia, there is concern about any slackening of effort and failure to grow, in order that the place of their "candlesticks" be not threatened (Rev. 2:5). Witness and growth must continue to the end, when the community of the redeemed from all nations gather around the throne for praise (Rev. 7:9-17) and serve the Lord "in his temple" (v. 15).

I submit, then, that the idea of a "churchless ministry" is unscriptural. Into what may the convert be incorporated if there is no fellowship? Our inheritance is a kingdom (Matt. 25:34) — a community concept. The offer of entity and of belonging implies man's need for something to which to belong. For this purpose the Lord builds his Church. If a "churchless ministry," in answer to the problems of the secular city, discards the church, it is also discarding Scripture, because Scripture commits believers to both the corporate group idea of the growing Church and the idea of belonging.

Scripture says nothing to me about any disappearance of the organic Church. Rather it seems to point in the opposite direction. I cannot see the victorious Christ without the Bride, or a biblical consummation without incorporating and belonging (Rev. 22:17). "To him be glory in the Church and in Christ Jesus to all generations, for ever and ever" (Eph. 3:20). In the New Testament, the word for Church is used either for the Church Universal (Eph. 3:21; 5:32, etc.), the Church at large (Gal. 1:1-3), or for a particular local church or congregation of believers (Phil. 4:15; Col. 4:15; Rom. 16:5, etc.). In any case, the permanence of the Church is basic to biblical thought, and the Christian is never conceptualized as an isolated person. He always belongs.

From the very beginning, the Church had some organic form, though it did not own buildings. There were the house churches (Rom. 16:5; I Cor. 16:19; Col. 4:15; Philem. v. 2). As the Christians increased in numbers, more and more were incorporated into the group (Acts 2:47), and some organic growth was inevitable if they were to be engaged in fellowship, instruction, prayers, and the breaking of bread — all corporate, not isolated acts (v. 42).

The First Letter to the Corinthians shows that the Church had already developed organically at an early date. Writing of the local church (14:23) and of the Church at large (12:27-8), as the Body of Christ, Paul shows organic growth with differentiation of functions and roles among the individual members (vv. 28-30). From this the discussion goes on to the matter of spiritual gifts and the demand for quality growth (ch. 13). There is no place here for a Christian in isolation. Although the individuals differ from each other, they belong to each other for the edification of the corporate Body (14:12,19,26).

PERFECTION GROWTH

Some church growth critics — usually superficial ones who have not really taken the trouble to ponder church growth terminology before criticizing it — say that church growth makes no allowance for *quality,* because it seeks a growth that is *quantitative.* The standard terminology was first defined by Dr. McGavran in *Bridges of God.* He differentiated between quantitative growth by conversion from paganism or from the world, which he called "discipling," and qualitative growth within the Church, which he called "perfecting." It must be insisted that both of these are essential to church growth theory, and each has its biblical base.

One might also add that, in the ever-growing data from field research, we have frequently discovered that persons who raise the "not quantity but quality" cliché use this self-defensively, in a way that suggests an unwillingness to face up to their own non-growth. Church growth research has no value unless those concerned are prepared to face the facts which the research reveals. Furthermore, in my own research I have been rather impressed by the disclosure that, time after time, quantitative, qualitative, and organic growth go together. They are often different manifestations of the same latent life and power.

This book would not be complete without some specific reference to the place of perfecting in church growth theory. The Bible has several things to say about it.

Jesus directed his followers to the importance of the process of perfecting or maturing, so that they might reflect the divine image (Matt. 5:48). Thinking of maturity in the office or role to which one is appointed, Paul stressed to Timothy that the man of God should be perfect (II Tim. 3:17). This not only applies to the Christian individual, but also to the collective "perfecting of the saints." In Ephesians we have a fine passage (4:11-12) that shows both the perfecting and organic growth of the corporate church together. Prophets, apostles, evangelists, pastors, and teachers are operating together for the perfecting of the saints, and for the edifying of the Body of Christ. The purpose of this edification is to bring all to "a knowledge of the Son of God" and to perfection (maturity), measured in terms of "the stature of the fullness of Christ" (v. 13), to be "no more children" (v. 14), but "growing into him in all things" (v. 15). This process of perfecting is conceptualized in terms of "the Body" (the Church) of which Christ is the Head, "increasing unto the edifying of itself in love" (v. 16).

The chapter goes on to distinguish between the old life and the new life in Christ. This is a common theme in the New Testament. Almost every book has something to say about the inner qualitative growth in grace that is expected of the Christian — both the individual and the group.

In spite of this, Christians can still fall into the trap of assuming that conversion is an *end* rather than a *beginning*. Movements from paganism into Christianity, especially large-scale movements within group structures or kin units, must be followed up pastorally and consummated. People-movements which have not stood up to the test of time have sometimes been cited as "faulty evangelism." Church growth research tends to suggest, however, that the fault is more frequently one of bad follow-up. It is not the discipling but the perfecting that is inadequate. People have turned from the old way but have not been built up in the new way. Instead of inner growth there is a void.

The Lord's parable of the man from whom he cast out the evil spirit (Luke 11:24-6) speaks to this very situation. Saved from his demon-possessed past, the man's life was not filled with a wholesome substitute. Because his soul was left empty, other spirits took up residence within him. The missionary and indigenous pastor are obligated to see that discipling is followed by perfecting, that, when evil is cast out, the convert is not left with a spiritual void. There must be growth in grace, growth to maturity. This is an essential part of church growth theory.

The benedictions of the New Testament books indicate clearly this need. Thus, the leaders of the early Church express their great desire that the Church may enjoy quality growth toward maturity. "Be perfect" is Paul's wish for the Corinthians in the second letter (13:11). "The very God of peace sanctify you wholly, and I pray God your whole spirit and soul and body be preserved blameless unto the coming of our Lord Jesus Christ" was his wish for the Thessalonians (I Thess. 5:23). Jude remembers the Church before him who "is able to keep you from falling, and to present you faultless" (v. 24). Peter asks that Jesus Christ may "make you perfect, stablish, strengthen, settle you" (I Pet. 5:10), and, in the second letter, he asks that the Church may "grow in grace and in the knowledge of our Lord and Saviour Jesus Christ" (3:18). In the Epistle to the Hebrews, the desire is that God will "make you perfect in every good work to do his will, working in you that which is well-pleasing in his sight, through Jesus Christ" (13:21).

In these benedictions the New Testament leaders ask God's blessing in bringing the congregations to maturity.

Discipling and perfecting, then, are different but related kinds of growth — one the quantitative intake due to evangelistic outreach, the other the qualitative development to maturity within the congregation. Without the former the congregation would die. Without the latter it would produce neither leaders nor mature members. Without maturity and leadership there would be no organic growth of "the Body."

If this book appears to emphasize discipling more than perfecting, this does not mean that the latter is less important. It rather indicates the writer's concern for the urgency of currently bringing men to Christ, who alone can bring them to maturity. We face an openness of the animistic world in our time, a readiness for change. There are many non-Christian advocates for the souls of men in competition with the Christian mission, and the day is far spent.

But let me reiterate that this does not in any way reduce the importance of perfection growth, the process which has as its inward aspect a growth in grace, and as its outward aspect Christian service, evangelical witness, and the fight for social justice (a matter often stressed in Scripture from the time of the eighth-century prophets).

By way of a final warning, however, there is an undesirable kind of "perfectionism" which must be avoided — a self-satisfied perfectionism which shuts off the congregation from the world, encloses it, and robs it of outreach. The congregation guilty of this is static. It is worse than static — it is dying. The marks of true perfection or maturity in Christ are the various forms of Christian outreach. This, it should be well noted, must be both individual and collective. The congregation will stand before judgment as much as the individual Christian. It is a tragic thing to discover a congregation which has failed to grow to maturity.

THE OUTREACHING CHURCH

The mission of the Church is out in the world. There is no place in church growth theory and theology for the enclosed congregation without outreach. When converts are incorporated into growing congregations, it is to strengthen them to go forth into the world again. Church growth theory is based on the mission and method of Jesus, which he transmitted to his followers.

Jesus saw his own incarnation in terms of a mission to the world: his coming from the Father, his birth as a human child, his human life experiences, his public ministry, his death on the cross, and his resurrection triumph were all part of his divine mission to the world and in the world (John 17:18; Luke 2:49; John 1:18, etc.).

Jesus called men to himself as disciples, either as pupils or apprentices, depending on how the Greek term is interpreted. But there was a point where Jesus began to treat them less as disciples and more as apostles ("sent ones"). At first this was probationary (Luke 10:1-20), but eventually the permanent commission was given (Matt. 28:19-20) in its right chronological position, when the full scope of the revelation of God in Jesus was clear before them. We see also that in the closing discourses of his earthly ministry Jesus pressed their mission upon them in terms of his own, indirectly in prayer (John 17:18), and more directly face to face (John 20:21).

Jesus' identification with the world had been complete — leaving the Father, entering the world, becoming man, even a servant, and dying a sinner's death on the cross (Phil. 2:5-8). His identification with man was *temporal,* at a point of historic time (Luke 2:1-2); *spatial,* set in a geographical location (v. 3); and *ethnic,* within the bounds of Jewish culture, specifically the Galilean subculture and in the lineage of David (v. 4). Through the lines of social structure, kin patterns, and daily occupations, Jesus identified with mankind in a human outreach. In the homes of the sick, by the lakeside, at social gatherings, he fraternized with people; but it was always to confront them with a word about the spiritual aspect of their salvation or a direct option for decision (Matt. 4:19; 8:22; 16:24; 19:21-2; Mark 2:14, etc.).

When the time came for him to depart, he committed to his followers the task that he had demonstrated during his lifetime (John 15:7-27). Witness also such phrases as "all things whatsoever I have commanded you" in the Great Commission.

Yet he knew the risk he took. Therefore, he warned them of their need to differentiate between his standards and those of the world. They were to be *in* the world but not *of* it, as he himself had been (John 15:18-9; 17:9-11,14-6. Cf. John 8:23); or, as Paul put it, they were to be *transformed* within the Roman environment, but not *conformed* to it (Rom. 12:1-2).

The method of Jesus was not to deny the validity of cultural structures but to present his challenge *within* them. His identification with publicans and sinners (Matt. 9:10-1) and with Samaritans (John 4:27) caused some comment from the ethnocentric Jews. His personal work with the woman of Samaria was not a case of casual individual evangelism; the Lord was establishing a contact to open his way into a village structure that was closed to him otherwise (John 4:39-40). The group won thereby was able to stand with mutual support, and this was better than one woman being left as a religious isolate (vv. 41-2).

The outreaching gospel was set before the earliest Christians in the figure of an ever-widening series of concentric circles — from Jerusalem to Judea, to Samaria, and to the uttermost parts of the earth (Acts 1:8).

While it is true that this outreaching ministry included Christian service, service projects were never an end in themselves. There was good theological reason for this. Although we are "created in Christ unto good works," good works alone do not lead to salvation, but to boasting; it is grace through faith that leads to growth (Eph. 2:8-9). Service projects without a gospel invitation tend to lead to merit theology and self-satisfaction or, as Paul calls it, boasting.

Yet the works can witness to the Lord as long as the appropriate testimony, or "appeal for belief," accompanies them. "Believe me," Jesus said, "for the very works' sake" (John 14:11). He was speaking of the works he was doing in the Father's name, for he was making the works demand belief. He was not offering them as a service project, as ends in themselves. We meet this issue on the mission field when service projects are mere "Christian presence." This is no better than Hindu merit theology. Unless the works demand belief in the one in whose name the service is rendered, this must surely lead to statistical boasting. It is as harmful to boast about quantitative food distributions as it is to vaunt the number of one's converts.

What then do we mean when we say that the Church is called to outreach into the world? The gospel outreach certainly includes service to fellow man: delivering captives, giving sight to the blind, setting the bruised at liberty. But this service is rendered with a preached gospel and a pastoral care (healing the broken-hearted). It was seen in these terms by Jesus at the outset of his ministry (Luke 4:18-9), and, after demonstrating this method for three years, he then commanded the apostles to go forth and demonstrate what he had taught them, to the ends of the world. This is the *outreaching* Church.

Finally, if there is to be an outreaching Church, there must be a body to organize and demonstrate this outreach. The process of going out was to bring in converts. Jesus spoke of other sheep who were to be brought into the flock (John 10:16). John, after two dogmatic verses of personal testimony, put it practically: the goal of his witness, and indeed of all Christian outreach, is to win men from the world into the joy of the fellowship (I John 1:3). With the joy of the fellowship in his heart, the convert is prepared to attend to his own outreach in the name which is above every name. Church growth requires an outreaching community. The congregation and its outreach stand or fall together. There is no place in church growth theory or theology for an enclosed congregation without outreach. This applies to evangelical mission, to service projects, and to the fight for social justice.

Organic Growth as Revitalization

The anthropologist Wallace, researching on social crises and stress situations, defines the process of "revitalization" as the reestablishment of social equilibrium in a society under stress. He describes the previous "steady state," the nature of the crisis, the dynamics of the changing situation, and the eventual emergence of a new steady state, so that the society is revitalized.

This is a process of organic or structural change. It has something to say to the organic renewal of the Church under stress. It may well be that a church or congregation is dying and needs renewal. That need may be spiritual or organic. The cure for the former is *revival*; the cure for the latter is *revitalization*. Revival is something that comes from without: it is the work of the Holy Spirit and may come unexpectedly. The Spirit may use some preacher, perhaps a stranger from outside; or it may begin in a prayer meeting. We can tabulate frequencies of revival and delineate some conditions that are frequently associated with it; but there is always something unpredictable about revivals. We cannot measure the work of the Spirit.

But revitalization is a renewal of the structure. It comes out of the crisis situation when the members of the society endeavor to deal with the crisis. It comes from within. It is a human program which can be observed, tested, and measured. Revival and revitalization are two separate processes and should be differentiated. In mission, revival links up with the divine resources, and revitalization restores organic structure by better techniques and methods of operation. Some critics of the church growth viewpoint have failed to make this distinction, perhaps because revival and revitalization so frequently go together.

Both revival and revitalization have direct bearing on both quantitative and qualitative church growth. The physical records of a church, if properly kept, should indicate this: increased evangelical outreach, better intake, good maturing, and rededication.

What does the Bible say about our responsibility in the renewal of the organic Church, the physical organization over which we have control as God's stewards? Certainly, both at home and abroad, many of our congregations are facing crises. Frequently they are more concerned with themselves rather than the needs of man, because they are fighting for their very existence. The old steady state has become a stress situation. The social anthropologist asks how a congregation will solve such a situation, that it might be revitalized. Are we to sit and wait for God to act with revival, or are we to take part in any program of renewal? Should the organic Church be restructured in any way to give it a greater potential for life in our day? With this question in mind, we turn to the New Testament.

The letters to the seven churches of Asia seem to present a situation similar to the one which we face. There is much for which they are commended, yet at many points they seem to be facing stress and crisis. It seems to me that the Lord expected them to take some definite action by way of renewal. He was holding them responsible for their organic functioning:

> Thou hast left thy first love. Remember therefore whence
> thou art fallen, and repent, and do the first works; or else

> I will come unto thee quickly, and will remove thy candle-
> stick.... (Rev. 2:4-5)

Furthermore, this word to Ephesus was to be passed on to the other churches, for this responsibility for congregational survival is a general principle (v. 7).

By looking at the seven letters together, we can reconstruct something of the total crisis in Asia at that time — doctrinal, moral, and social. The letters suggest that the Lord expected them to be responsible, to face the situation realistically, and to overcome. Solve the stress situation, revitalize the church, overcome! Look over those letters and pick out the word "overcome" (Rev. 2:7,11,17,26; 3:5,12,21, and cf. 21:7). Here is expressed the necessity of the congregation's own effort at organic renewal.

The organic structure of the Church is not simple. Even in the earliest records, once there were house churches, house to house visitation, the breaking of bread, fellowship meals, gatherings for praise and testimony, and steady numerical growth (Acts 2:46-7), the complexity of the organic Church was inevitable. Organization and the use of officials were soon required. Read Romans 12:5-13, and consider the basic organic differentiations within the Body of Christ.

From the very start, the structure was dynamic and not static. New programs were required as well as institutionalized officials to carry them out; and these often came out of stress situations. The process of revitalization is built into the New Testament Church. Acts 6 shows what this means. Here was a stress situation: the steady state of the young Church was thrown into stress (v. 1). The whole congregation assembled to face the crisis realistically (v. 2). A solution was devised which led to a basic organic change that has influenced the Church down to this day — namely, the recognition of specialization in order to satisfy both proclamation and service. Thus the group overcame the stress situation that threatened to disrupt the Church, and a new steady state was achieved. In this organic renewal the Church went ahead to further quantitative growth, even to the winning of a number of Jewish priests (v. 7). This is a good example of the process of revitalization. We note in passing that the apostles did make the occasion a matter of prayer (v. 6). They acted "under God," but they themselves had to take the initiative. We also note that, in this case at least, there appears to have been some direct relationship between organic growth and quantitative intake.

Today, Christian supporters of missions do not need a social anthropologist to point out that many churches or congregations are facing serious crises. Many are fighting for existence. This is a subject for a whole book. If we were to write such a book, we would classify these dying churches for purposes of study. There would be the congregations of third or fourth generation mission churches still dependent on foreign funds, that have never been treated as anything but children, and over whom paternalism still hovers like a Los Angeles smog. There is another type exclusively enclosed, self-satisfied, without any evangelistic outreach, and the service it renders is given without direct contact. Still another is tied by forms so archaic that rapport with the world is impossible. Some have lost "the spiritual glow" (Rom. 12:11, Moffatt version); some have lost hold of the truth (Gal. 3:1-3); some are more concerned with theological controversy than with bringing men to Christ. These churches are in danger of losing their candlesticks.

Revitalization must come from within the congregation. God expects us to take stock of our shortcomings and adjust our ways. Church growth has much to say for this dimension of church activity. Special study is made of methods and techniques. We know that the Church requires an organic structure with a potential for life. Our case studies suggest that God does undoubtedly bless those congregations who care for their organic growth just as in the case we have examined from Acts 6. "Examine yourselves," said Paul to the Corinthians. "Prove your own selves. . . . Be perfect, be of good comfort, be of one mind, live in peace" (II Cor. 13:5,11). A church has to be growing organically to achieve this holy living. But the Lord has placed the organic Church in our care and has made us responsible, so that "the brethren may dwell together in unity" (Psa. 133:1). To some extent, both quantitative and qualitative growth depend on our faithfulness.

THE CHRISTIAN MISSION SET IN TIME

One hears a voice which says that life has changed so dramatically in these postwar years, that the day of Christian mission is dead. This book is devoted to the examination of missionary concepts in the light of Scripture; therefore, I raise the question: *is the view that the Christian mission is dying in these changing times compatible with Scripture?*

The Christian mission is set in time and has certain specific marks: *historicity, continuity,* and *finality.*

The Old Testament promises, Jesus assured the congregation at Nazareth, "are fulfilled in your ears" (Luke 4:21). The evangelist records that "the Word became flesh and dwelt among us" (John 1:14), and he was supported by Paul, who thought of the divine initiative in terms of "the fullness of time" (Gal. 4:4; Eph. 1:10). We are not, as in some religions, handling poetry and ideas but historical events and statements. This can only be escaped by a changed view of the Bible.

It was in history that the Lord came with his mission from the Father, as he is so frequently recorded as having said in the Fourth Gospel (5:37; 6:38-40,57; 7:28-9; 8:16; 17:21; 20:21, etc.). The death on the cross for the sin of man, which spells out salvation for any, or all, or everyone, or whosoever will to believe, is again rooted in statements regarded as historical by the biblical writers.

The resurrection, the power of which is available for believers, is also recorded as history (Phil. 3:10). Furthermore, after Christ's physical departure, it was by another historic event that the disciples were made aware of the truth that they had entered the times of the Holy Spirit (Acts 2). Prior to this, the commission to Christian mission in the world (John 17:18) and to the world (Matt. 28:19) was historically recorded in time and place.

So the Church is historically (not poetically or mythically) commissioned to bring men to Christ, to incorporate them into congregations or fellowships (I John 1:3), and to care for their growth in grace (II Pet. 3:18). For this quantitative growth once again we have a limited number of genuine historical reference points. What lay between Peter's commission, "Feed my sheep" (John 21:17) and his advice to the elders years later,

"Feed the flock of God" (I Pet. 5:1-2)? These historic charges called for a *continuity* of effort.

Jesus had suggested the responsibility for continuity in his preaching. The lost sheep, the lost coin, and the lost son remind us not only of the tragedy of lostness but the continuous need for bringing sinners to repentance (Luke 15:7,10,32). The shepherd, the woman, and the father never rested or slackened their concern until the lost was found. The whole imagery of the role of the disciple suggests life involvement, continuity of responsibility to the endless mission and ministry. They were to be fishers of men (Matt. 4:19), good soldiers of Jesus Christ (II Tim. 2:3), and stewards of his grace (I Pet. 4:10).

As with disciples, so with churches: the commission to mission and ministry must go on. The letters to the seven churches in Asia (Rev. 2,3) reveal the deep-seated danger of the loss of continuity in witness and the possibility of having one's candlestick removed from its place (Rev. 2:5).

Is there any end to this commission to mission and ministry? Is there any point of *finality* in time? The phrase used by the early Christians was "until the day of Christ" or "until the coming of the Lord Jesus Christ." Only then is there finality. Congregations were given the blessing in this terminology (I Thess. 5:23; Phil. 1:6), and individual Christians, when appointed to posts of responsibility, were charged to faithful service in these terms (I Tim. 6:14). Furthermore, the Great Commission itself implied this when those commissioned were promised the divine presence "even unto the end of the world" (Matt. 28:20). The early Christians appear to have understood that the Lord's commission to mission and ministry was continuous until his return — "to all generations, for ever and ever" (Eph. 3:20).

It is interesting to notice that the much-discussed Vatican II documents say, in the "Decree on the Missionary Activity of the Church," "the time for missionary activity extends between the first coming of the Lord and the second." This is the biblical point of view. The finality in mission comes only when the Lord has returned. As the Bible explains it, this is the Christian mission *set in time*.

It is not right to assume that because we live in times of rapid cultural change the need for mission is past or the opportunity for it closed. We may need to change the forms and techniques for presenting the Christian mission to suit our times; but the Bible says that this Christian mission was commissioned in history, is continuous through history, and finds finality only when history itself comes to an end.

V

Church Growth and the Christian Hope

THE PROMISES OF GOD

By what authority do I write with such certainty of expectation? I have sought to present what one can learn from the written Word, in the name of him who stands behind that Word. The promises are of the Lord. I write, like Luke, "that thou mightest know the certainty" (Luke 1:4). In order fully to know this certainty, we must collect the biblical data about the promises of God.

The "promise" and the "promises" are biblical terms. Although they often refer to specific promises of the Lord made in Old Testament times, and especially to Abraham, yet they are mainly New Testament terms, from the Gospels and the life and letters of the New Testament Church. The early Christian Church claimed ownership of those promises. The degree to which this is true becomes apparent when one discovers that Abraham is mentioned seventy-five times in the New Testament, and quite frequently his name is coupled with a reference to the promise(s).

The Letter to the Hebrews speaks of "inheriting the promises" (6:12), "receiving the promises" (10:36) and of the "promise of eternal inheritance" (9:15). We cannot do without the Old Testament, because it provides the historical matrix in which many of these promises were made — the forward look, first to the coming of Christ and subsequently to the eternal inheritance through faith in Christ. As the first volume of the history of man's salvation, the Old Testament states the aims and goals of the scriptural pilgrimage.

74

Abraham is depicted in the New Testament as a model of faith (Rom. 4:13,16,20, etc.). In the New Testament Church, the promises to Abraham are seen as being transmitted to all men of true faith through Christ. This is the promise of the Spirit to all of Abraham's seed — i.e., true believers who are ready to act on their belief (Gal. 3:14,22). Abraham is a New Testament symbol. The fact that he was a patriarchal, nomadic tent-dweller, and as far removed as possible from the citizens of the Galatian towns, does not prevent the Galatians from sharing his promises. Faith can penetrate cultural barriers. This is why the doctrine of the promises of God is integral to the missionary program.

Paul was much concerned with this transmission of the faith to Gentiles, not only to the Galatians but also to the Romans (the Roman Church seems to have contained Romans as well as Greeks). This concern is seen particularly in an interesting unit of the Epistle to the Romans, in which he cites four Old Testament passages in four verses (Rom. 15:8-19. See vv. 9-12). To the Ephesians also he spoke of the Gentiles' being "partakers of the promises in Christ by the gospel" (Eph. 3:6).

The subject matter of the promises was further developed in the New Testament period. By collecting the scriptural references to the promises of God, I find that they fall into four classes.

(1) Some of the promises of Old Testament prophecy were realized in the coming of Christ. This is implied in the New Testament's manner of citing from the Old Testament to support biblical descriptions and discussions of the life and work of our Lord. It is more specific in Acts, where Luke mentions the incarnation (Acts 12:23) and the resurrection (13:32-33) in terms of the promises of God.

(2) Paul the missionary saw his own call as "by the will of God according to the promise of life which is in Christ Jesus" (II Tim. 1:1). The promise of salvation is open to all: "this is the promise he hath promised us, even eternal life" (I John 2:25), or as James put it, "receiv(ing) the crown of life, which the Lord hath promised to them that love him" (1:12), and again "heirs of the kingdom, which he hath promised to them that love him" (2:5). In this category we see the promises of

God to man, unlimited promises with respect to salvation, and assurances to the faithful.

(3) Then there are promises concerning the Holy Spirit. First, Pentecost itself was a fulfillment of promise (Luke 24:49; Acts 1:4; 2:33). This is in line with the Lord's own assurance of the coming of the Comforter (John 14:16). Although the actual word "promise" is not used in this passage, it is used in all the other references I have cited in this chapter. The promise of the Spirit is not confined to the original disciples, but is also for their "children" and "to them that are afar off, even as many as the Lord our God shall call," as stated in Peter's Pentecostal sermon (Acts 2:39). This is a missionary insight from the day of Pentecost.

(4) That part of the Christian hope which bears on the final consummation is also included in the contents of the promise of God. "We, according to the promises," said Peter (II Pet. 3:13), "look for new heavens and a new earth, wherein dwelleth righteousness." Paul spoke of "the Holy Spirit of promise" (Eph. 1:13), a pledge and foretaste of something fuller to come for those who believe. In presenting the Christian hope to Agrippa, Paul showed it as springing from Jewish conceptual roots. He presented Christ as "the hope of the promise made of God unto our fathers" (Acts 26:6). Here again we see that the New Testament is taking over the Old Testament promises and concentrating them in Christ. In Christ these promises may be realized by those who believe.

I have never seen a theology book that develops the idea of the promises of God as doctrine, but we have all the material for it in Scripture. Furthermore, the Greek word used in all these passages for "promise" means "proclamation." It covers both the fact of proclamation and the message proclaimed. In I John 1:5, the word is translated as message. What we have here is a divine declaration. The Bible does not say, "These things are put up for your consideration." We are not in the realm of argument or reason; there is something dogmatic about a proclamation. If we accept the Bible as our rule for faith and practice, we are dealing with the sure word of God about our spiritual situation and our eternal hope.

The most common feature of all these promises of God is the

direct statement or implication of some specific relationship between these promises and the faith of man. The work of God in Christ, the work of the Holy Spirit, and the Christian hope of eternal life are all available to men who, like Abraham, are prepared both to believe and to act on that belief. Abraham is symbolically the father of all men of faith and action.

The missionary dimension of this truth (and this is where it particularly speaks to church growth theory) is that the Christian Church takes over the promises made to Israel, because they are realized in Christ. Furthermore, they are enlarged on such a scale as to incorporate the Gentiles as "partakers of the promises in Christ by the gospel" (Eph. 3:6). The Holy Spirit also is available to "all that are afar off" (Acts 2:39). Thus, the Christian program of church-planting is found to be within the promises and proclamations of God. When we set the promises of God beside the Great Commission, we have both assurances and directives that are compellingly powerful.

THE CHURCH AND THE CONSUMMATION

We began with a study of diffusion. We saw that the prophetic idea of the earth becoming "full of the knowledge of the Lord as the waters cover the sea" (Isa. 11:9) called for a program and process that continues until it is accomplished. The present-day Church is involved. Church growth and the diffusion of the gospel go together. Now we conclude our biblical pilgrimage with a glance at the end, which the Bible encourages us to anticipate. We turn to the visions of the Book of Revelation, especially chapters 7 and 21-22.

These lead us to expect a gathering together, when the saints will see their essential unity in Christ (Rev. 7:9). Whether these descriptions are to be taken as literal or allegorical is not the point; they seem to say certain things clearly: the Church will experience the true oneness it has never really known on earth; its divisions will disappear and great will be the joy of fellowship with the Lord of Glory. Let us now look at some of the key features of our expectations.

(1) It is true that each individual Christian ("he who overcometh," 21:7) has something to look forward to with excitement, because he will discover new dimensions of his

relationship with Christ as Savior and King (7:14-17), and meet him face to face (22:4; cf. I Cor. 13:12). However, the strongest feature of the visions of the Revelation is their corporate emphasis. The joy and worship is corporate throughout. The kindreds and tribes and tongues, apparently retaining in some way their distinctive entities, are yet one before the Lord of Glory (7:9; 21:24,26); national differences and discords are healed (22:2) and sorrows ended (21:4).

(2) A significant role is given to the Church in the messianic kingdom to come, and at the very end of the Bible we are told that these visions of consummation and judgment are "to be testified in the churches" (22:16), suggesting some relationship between the Church eternal and glorified and the churches on earth. The churches are to be warned of the choice between life and death, and the messenger of the Lord is to present this option. This is the missionary imperative for all time and the importance of church growth on earth in our day.

(3) The symbol of the Church in glory (also described in the figure of the New Jerusalem) is that of the "Bride of Christ," and the consummation of history is seen in terms of the bridal feast of the Lamb (21:2,9; 22:17). With respect to the first figure, there is no church building in the city, so the Holy City is itself the Church (21:22). The Church is holy to the Lord. With respect to the second figure, the Church is presented worthy, as a bride adorned for her husband. The idea of a bridal feast offers a high concept of fellowship. This corporate fellowship was suggested first by Jesus himself when he instituted the Holy Communion and spoke of another communion to come in the kingdom (Luke 22:16,18). Horatius Bonar captured this identification of the Lord and his disciples on earth with the communion to come in glory:

> Feast after feast thus comes and passes by,
>   Yet passing, points to that glad feast above,
> Giving sweet foretaste of the festal joy,
>   The Lamb's great bridal feast of bliss and love.

This is another reason why church-planting must go on, that converts may be introduced to the warmth of communion, the foretaste of that which is to come.

(4) The features emphasized as the marks of the Church to come seem to be:

- (i) a common experience of salvation from sin, through Christ (Rev. 7:13-4);
- (ii) a common confession of Christ as Triumphant Lord of History, both in personal (21:7) and communal life (7:9; 21:24);
- (iii) a common fellowship in praise and adoration (7:11-12).

The question now arises: how is such a community to be brought about? I believe it is God's will to bring it about through his Church; otherwise why must the vision be reported in the churches (22:16)? Just as the Holy Spirit is given here on earth as an earnest (a pledge and foretaste) of the glory to come (Eph. 1:12-14), so is the Church an anticipatory institution. God has permitted us foresight, through these visions, to see something of what we may expect of the heavenly community — corporate, not individual but multi-individual, sharing the salvation experience through faith in the slain Lamb, now enthroned, and worshipping in a fellowship of common confession, praise, and adoration.

Where, on earth, can a man be prepared for such an experience? Does not this both set an ideal for the Church on earth and provide her with a directive? Are we not moving in the right direction when we go and make disciples, when we plant churches among the nations and tribes and kindred and tongues? Does not the Great Commission lead us on in the spiritual pilgrimage and program that is most anticipatory of the heavenly consummation?

Finally, there is the matter of the continuity of the invitation to men to share this experience to the very end. The Holy Spirit pleads with men. The Church presents the Evangel. Every Christian convert is urged to be a missionary.

> The Spirit and the Bride say, Come.
> Let him that heareth say, Come.

But there must be a response:

> Let him that is athirst come. And whosoever will, let him take the water of life freely. (Rev. 22:17)

To this end we plant churches on earth and strive for church growth, that his name alone may be praised and the day of his kingdom brought near.

Index

Acceptance and rejection, 14, 20-25, 31, 32, 37-40, 43, 53-54
Acculturation, 34

Baptism, 24-25, 33, 53, 59
Believing, 20-25, 31, 40, 53-54, 75-77
Belonging, 36, 58-61

Church
   assembly, 7
   body of Christ, 7, 61, 62, 63, 69
   bride of Christ, 50, 60, 78, 79
   fellowship, 8, 11, 12, 13, 25, 31, 67, 71, 77, 78, 79
   household of God, 59
Churches, house, 7, 30, 69
Church growth
   organic, 7, 13, 33, 60, 61, 62, 67-70
   qualitative, 7, 12, 14, 24, 26-27, 61, 68, 71
   quantitative, 7, 12, 13, 14, 15-17, 26-27, 61, 68, 69-70, 71
Church planting, 11, 77, 78
Clark, Sidney, 25
Commission, the Great, 8, 11, 25, 30, 32, 50, 65, 79
Communication, 13, 28, 44
Confessing, 20-25, 79
Congregation(s), 7, 8, 11, 31, 58, 64, 67-70, 71
Consolidation, 25
Consummation, 11, 30, 50, 77-80
Context, 33-37

Continuity, 25-27, 38, 71-72, 79
Conversion, 19-25, 31-33, 36, 44, 62

Decision-making, 31-33, 37-40, 65
Diffusion, 7, 10-12, 77
Discipling, 25-27, 33, 55, 61

Elders, 7, 33, 54, 71
Encounter, 12, 32, 38, 40, 44
Evidence
   cumulative, 9, 14
   declarative, 9
   implicative, 9, 15
   precedential, 9
Expectation, 10, 11, 12, 13, 41, 74

Factor, the divine, 42-46
Faith, transmission of the, 74-77
Faithfulness, 40-41, 70
Function, differentiation of, 56, 61

Grace, prevenient, 46
Group, 12, 14, 32, 35, 38
   corporate, 7, 59
   social and ethnic, 22-23, 30, 31-33
Group experience, 12
Group movements, see people movements
Growth, imagery of, 10, 12-15

Harvest, 18, 26, 41, 43-44, 46, 48, 53, 56
Historicity, 7, 71
Holy Spirit, 8, 9, 20, 31, 32, 33, 34, 38, 39, 43, 44, 45, 46, 49, 51-52, 67, 71, 75, 76, 77, 79

81

Identification, Christ's, 65
Idols, 10, 40, 49
Incorporating, 8, 10, 11, 12, 13, 25, 40-42, 58-61, 71
Ingathering, 25, 48, 53
Inheritance, 48-49, 53, 74, 75-77
Interaction, 13
Invitation, 50, 79

Justice, social, 12, 64
Judgment, 52, 53, 64, 78

Location, strategic, 52-54
Lostness, state of, 21, 22, 24, 49-50, 72

"Mass movement," 31
McGavran, Donald, 6, 25, 26, 61
Merit theology, 66
Ministry, churchless, 58, 60
Mission, 8, 10, 12, 19-25, 37, 39, 48, 54-57, 71-73
Motivation, 15-17, 23, 29
Multi-individual decision, 31-33
Multi-individual society, 79

Nations, 10, 11, 50, 53
Numbering, 15-17

Obedience, 10, 15, 18-19
Obstruction, 50-52
Opportunity, 31, 49
Ordination, 33
Outreach, 26, 55, 64-67

Pentecost, 8, 20, 22, 32, 51, 76
Penetration, 13, 14
People movements, 20, 23, 33, 44, 61
People of God, 28, 31, 32, 47
Perfecting, 26-27, 33, 55, 56, 61-64
Perfectionism, 64

Possessions, 47-50
Prayer, 12, 56-57, 70
Presence, Christian, 12, 24, 50, 56, 66
Proclamation, 39-40, 49
Promises of God, 7, 8, 11, 47, 71, 74-77
Purpose, divine, 7, 10, 32, 51

Repenting, 20-25, 31, 58
Responsibility, 8, 10, 18-19, 24, 29, 32, 41, 46, 50, 51, 59, 68, 69, 71
Return of the Lord, 26-27, 72-73
Revitalization, 67-70
Revival, 67-68
Rice-Christians, 34, 36
Roles, functional, 33, 40-42, 45

Self-glorification, 15
Service, 12, 26, 39, 51, 52, 54-57, 64, 66
Shearer, Roy E., 6
Social structure, 14, 15, 28-31, 34, 44, 62
Statistics, 15-17, 19, 24, 66
Stewardship, 17, 18, 41, 56, 68, 72
Stress situations, 67-70

Time, 44, 71-73
Turning to the Lord, 20-25

Verdict, 24, 39, 55-56, 57

Warneck, G., 10
Watching, 56-57
Wesley, John, 20, 46
Winnability, 30-31
Witness, 8, 14, 37, 39, 40, 60, 64, 67, 72
Worship, 10, 11, 31, 32, 50, 58, 60, 78

DATE DUE